BOTTLENECK BREAKTHROUGH

BOTTLENECK BREAKTHROUGH

How to Find & Fix Your #1 Business Challenge To Unlock
Sustainable Growth, Fast

Published in the United States by Bottleneck Breakthrough Group.
www.BottleneckBreakthrough.com

Library of Congress Cataloging-in-Publication Data
Long, Joshua
1. Small Business   2. Entrepreneurship   3. Management

ISBN   978-1-61961-719-3 Hardcover
        978-1-61961-720-9 Ebook

Cover design by GRATICLE DESIGN
Editing by ARGUS EDITORIAL
Layout design by BOOKINABOX.COM

FIRST EDITION
Printed in the United States of America
10 9 8 7 6 5 4 3 2 1

BOTTLENECK
BREAK
THROUGH

HOW TO FIND & FIX YOUR #1 BUSINESS CHALLENGE TO UNLOCK SUSTAINABLE GROWTH, FAST

JOSHUA LONG

CONTENTS

Preface i

Foreword iii

1. The Bottleneck 1

LEVER #1. STRATEGY **17**

2. The Big Idea 19

3. Optimization 33

LEVER #2. MARKETING **47**

4. Your Funnel 49

5. Traffic Pillars 67

6. Closing 87

LEVER #3. MANAGEMENT **103**

7. Management Basics 105

8. Weekly Implementation Meeting 123

9. Confrontation 139

LEVER #4. SYSTEMS **157**

10. Systemize It 159

11. Delegate, Document & Automate 171

LEVER #5. VISION **187**

12. What's The Goal? 189

13. Bottleneck Breakthrough Plan 203

LEVER #6. MINDSET **223**

14. Getting Free 225

Acknowledgements 243

Preface

If you're anything like my clients, you're sitting on a goldmine waiting to be dug up. But the endless stream of books, seminars, and new fads is so strong that your treasure is buried and hidden. This book is the map you've been praying for.

You can throw away every "silver bullet" gimmick you've accumulated. Your business is stuck because you have bottlenecks clogging things up, and you can break through them right now.

What you will learn from this book is how the problems keeping you up at night can be easily solved by pulling each of the *6 Growth Levers* I give you. Yes, even the problems that cause you to abandon your most important relationships and damage your body from stress, drinking, or other attempts at self-medicating.

None of this is rocket science. It's possible you might not learn anything new in this book. But if you follow the system I teach, your business and personal life will improve exponentially. I know this because I've done it for dozens of businesses of all sizes and industries. Every single time, without exception, my clients have experienced an improvement in their businesses by using the exact same framework I teach you in this book.

Let me encourage you to actually read AND implement the things you learn here.

Go to *www.bbg.li/guide* and enter your email to receive a completely customized, action-focused, weekly email from me that adjusts to the pace you're reading through the book.

The last thing I want is for this book to collect dust on your bookshelf. So I created something I've never seen before with this advanced guided-coaching email series to help you cut through the noise of the day-to-day, and actually read about AND implement the *Bottleneck Breakthrough Method* in your business.

If meteoric growth and scale isn't your goal, everything in this book works just as well to streamline what you already have so you're making more profit from less effort. Most importantly, it will help reduce your stress by strengthening your business, regardless of its size.

Now, read the Foreword by my past client and good friend Benjamin Gorelick to see how the *Bottleneck Breakthrough Method* transformed his business and life immediately.

Foreword

You'd think the afternoon I spent, shotgun in my lap, debating whether I should splatter my brains on the wall above my bed would represent the low point of my life.

On the table in the next room was a stack of bills that would never get paid as my business churned inexorably toward bankruptcy. Downstairs, my employees went about their daily routine, oblivious to the man sobbing just above them.

In many ways, however, that was the best day of my life, because I chose life. I know now what I discovered then: Apparently I'm not a quitter. No matter how bad things get, I'll suffer through it, because tomorrow is another day, and with that new day comes a bit of hope.

No, the low point came a few years later. The business had been consolidated. Financial balance had been restored. Staff had been trimmed.

We had been profitable for about six quarters in a row at that point and those dark days really were behind me. Yet, I would still wake up every morning knowing that today wasn't going to be any better than the last. I'd work 14 hours, mostly putting out fires, go to sleep, and repeat. I was so overwhelmed with "stuff" to do, I could hardly think straight, much less take the time needed to actually solve the problems that plagued my business. There wasn't enough time in the day, and on those few days when there were enough hours, there wasn't enough energy.

By this point, my business had been around for eight years. In that time, I'd gone through nine managers. Oddly, they didn't want to spend 14 hours a day working on my business. I'd spent countless thousands on marketing advice, webinars, mastermind groups, online chat groups, and the like from the gurus of the industry.

None of them addressed the problem I had. I was caught in a terrible cycle.

I had grown the business three times, and each time it grew bigger than I could handle by myself, I got buried, then contracted the business so I could get a handle on things again.

It wasn't that I wasn't good at my job. I was quite capable of growing the business. I'd taken to AdWords and Facebook advertising pretty quickly, and I had a steady stream of prospects and customers. Even the suicide-inducing version of things mentioned above would have been a really great position for us, if only I were able to work 44 hours a day.

Simply put, I kept hitting this barrier, around $1 million a year, where I couldn't do everything myself. I'd hire someone to help out, they'd burn out in about six months, and I'd be left to clean up the mess they dropped into my lap on their way out the door. And after eight years, it all felt hopeless. Sure, I was capable of suffering along for the ride, but what kind of life is that?

That was the low point of my life.

And it was that depression that Josh Long stepped into with his *Bottleneck Breakthrough Method*.

Josh will probably spend the rest of this book telling you how easy the *Bottleneck Breakthrough Method* is to apply. It's not. Not because it's complicated or particularly onerous. It's pretty simple, analyzing six levers around which your business revolves and then making the small changes necessary to make a big difference. It really is a simple concept.

No, the challenge is that the process requires introspection. It requires a level of honesty with yourself that you may not be comfortable with. It requires that you accept your strengths and weaknesses, that you accept yourself for who you are. Instead of fighting yourself, the goal is to fill in the gaps either through systemization or hiring the right people.

I'm sure it'll come as a surprise to you, knowing a bit about things, that most of my business's strengths and weaknesses involved me. To solve the business's problems, I just had to solve the "me" problems, get out of my own way, and trust the process.

The very first thing Josh did with the business was to help us better understand the strengths and weaknesses of everyone on staff, myself included. From there, we moved most of the folks around, to places where they'd actually succeed. My new manager had, two days previously, been an intern I'd hired because her boyfriend was my previous manager, and she needed something to do for the summer. She was in charge of landscaping the building. Seriously. Her boyfriend, previously the manager, was moved to sales. I fired myself from all the money stuff, from all the logistics, and from sales. I fired my wife altogether.

In total, we moved fourteen people from one place to another, about two-thirds of my staff.

Then we set about writing job descriptions for everyone so they all knew what success would look like.

I invested my time, ruthlessly, in making myself redundant to the day-to-day tasks. As I came across something I needed to do to put out a fire, I'd train someone else to put out the fire. And then they were put in charge of handling the problem from that day forward.

We twiddled around with our payment schedules for customers, making them much more strict, since Josh showed me that I was a pushover there. We made everything a little more expensive, and then we cut the stuff that just didn't make money or caused a disproportionate amount of headaches.

Really, none of it was complicated. A few phone calls between Josh and me to apply the *Bottleneck Breakthrough Method*, look at a few spreadsheets, and then make some changes here and there.

In the end, I'd say we made six changes to the business over an eighteen-month period that really moved things for us. No one change required more than four hours of work to discover, identify, and solve. The trick was identifying the problems, the heart of it, and swallowing my pride or dispelling my preconceived notions of what "ought to be done."

I'm eternally grateful for the system/organization that Bottleneck Breakthrough provided. Because it is objective, you can't really argue with what it says you should do. Equally, that objective system makes it easier to accept. It doesn't matter how something "feels" to you. There's no personal judgment. No *"You're a failure because you xyz or didn't abc."* It's just a series of *"Hey, we did this test, and the evidence says your business will be more efficient/stronger/better if you do this."*

Find the bottleneck. Break through.

Easy peasy.

It's been about 3 years since I started working with Josh and, yeah, Bottleneck Breakthrough is still working. We've grown well past the $1 million ceiling we kept smacking against. We'll do just under $4 million this year. My gardener/intern-turned-manager is still the manager. I joke that she pretty much runs the place, but it's only half a joke. I finally get to spend 80 percent of my time working on big picture stuff that makes the business better, stronger, and capable of growing for the future.

I'm still imperfect and so is the business. But it's a hell of a lot better than it was.

The crippling anxiety is gone, and even though I've flown 147,386 miles this year to lead the business, I'm more fulfilled than ever before.

Mostly, it feels great to be hopeful again. To be grateful. To be engaged and challenged and to spend my fourteen hours of work a day doing things that I find meaningful.

I love my job and the path my life has taken—a path I wouldn't have found without Bottleneck Breakthrough.

—*Benjamin Gorelick*
MOUNTAIN TRAINING SCHOOL

CHAPTER I

The Bottleneck

"MOST PEOPLE SPEND MORE TIME AND
ENERGY GOING AROUND PROBLEMS THAN IN
TRYING TO SOLVE THEM."

—*Henry Ford*

Thirty minutes until the plane lands and Tim can finally get home to unwind for a day or two over the weekend. Maybe he'll shoot over to the beach house tonight to make the most of it. What's the point of owning it anyway if he never uses it?

The week-long trip to meet with two worthwhile prospects and a longstanding, high-maintenance client seems to be the norm now. At least that's how it feels since Tim is the best closer in his company, outpacing his entire sales team and both of his partners combined.

Running a $20 million company was supposed to be more glamorous and fulfilling than the struggling startup from 25 years ago. That was what he convinced himself of when merging with his two partners nearly a decade ago.

Now, it seems the only way to really get what he wants from this business is to keep the throttle down to grow profits so they can get acquired by another company, allowing Tim to bail out with his pile of cash.

Like so many business owners that have succeeded at creating a sustainable business, one that manages to pay the bills month-in and month-out, Tim is trapped on a hamster wheel. He's gone from being an innovator to being a closer and manager. And like most business owners, he's discovered that closing doesn't bring the rush it used to and managing the day-to-day business grew old a long time ago.

Every business goes through this pattern, assuming they survive long enough. It's the classic trap of success, achieving what so few can, only to be stuck in the end doing what you never really wanted to do. And like most business owners, Tim is trapped, flying to every corner of the country and putting out fires that should have been prevented in the first place.

Tim's manufacturing company is stuck at a plateau. Every business in every industry hits them. And they come at fairly similar stages.

For Tim, it's at $20 million right now. And like most businesses that have stalled on a plateau, the business has been there for a few years.

If Tim were reading another book, like *Built to Sell* by John Warrilow, he'd focus on reducing the options they offer clients so sales and fulfillment could be streamlined. Michael Gerber of *The E-Myth* would have him focus on documenting all of their systems so his staff would serve clients more effectively by having checklists to follow for most of their day-to-day tasks.

As an experienced business growth consultant I agree with these general principles, which have been proven to work over the years, helping to solve problems that are common in many businesses. In fact, I often recommend them to my clients and will discuss them at various points in this book.

Instead of a blanket prescription that will generally help every business at every stage of growth, I prefer a specific solution that hits the bull's-eye, creating as much of an improvement as possible with the least amount of effort and risk. That creates leverage.

So let's find the levers that move your business mountains. The levers that matter.

The single most reliable method I've found to uncover these levers is finding and fixing the bottlenecks in your business. The great news is that you can learn to do this to unlock massive growth or make your business run more smoothly without you.

Bottleneck Hunting

A bottleneck is any point of friction in your business that prevents you from generating more revenue or generating the same revenue more easily. When I talk about bottlenecks, business owners always ask for examples of what they look like so they can find them in their own business. There will be plenty of examples throughout this book, along with checklists and tools online at *BottleneckBreakthrough.com/book.**

For young companies, the most common bottleneck occurs when the owner no longer has the capacity to keep everything

---

* The shortlink *bbg.li* will be used throughout the book to make sure links are always current and easier to type out.

running. Crossing the chasm from doing everything herself to finding someone she can trust and then delegating to them can be a daunting challenge.

Then there are companies right at the $1 million plateau.[*] They've got a good team in place, and the owner is out making deals and keeping everyone fed, but he's probably holding back on closing as much as he could because he knows the overflow would fall back on his shoulders.

In both of these cases, there are clear, proven steps the business owner can take to remove these bottlenecks and unlock more growth. This type of growth can be very fast, occurring in the *6 Growth Levers*, which we will cover thoroughly in this book.

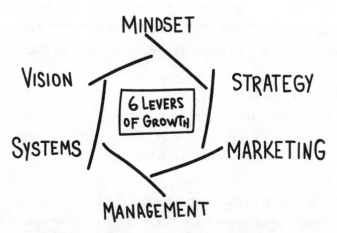

As we go through each section, you'll learn to see each bottleneck and how to fix it. Plus, you'll develop the foundation for a very powerful skill in the process. Master this one skill, and

---

[*]   Refer to the Bottleneck Matrix on page 6 to see the most common bottlenecks at each stage.

you'll be in the top 1 percent of business owners in the world that grow companies, instead of simply owning a job.

Breaking through bottlenecks is the most effective path you'll find to create sustainable growth. I'm talking about the kind of growth that makes your life easier and increases the value of your business at the same time.

As for Tim, not having a Director of Sales who can level up the sales team is his bottleneck right now. The return from investing in talented sales leadership won't pay off immediately, but within six to twelve months the momentum will be visible. By this time next year, Tim will have cut his travel time in half while watching revenue break through the current plateau. Plus, he'll spend more weekends at the beach house.

Theory of Constraints

After seeing the power of fixing bottlenecks in a business, I was pleased to find that it was similar to the theory of constraints proposed by Eli Goldratt in his book *The Goal*. Goldratt was attempting to refocus manufacturing production in the early 1980s when manufacturers were obsessed with efficiency at every stage of the process. You might be wondering what could possibly be the problem with making everything as efficient as possible? The problem lies in the fact that certain stages of production are more time-consuming or costly than other stages.

For example, a cell phone has a number of parts (screen, microphone, case, processor, etc.) that need to be produced. Before Goldratt came into the picture, the manufacturer would aim to make each step of the process as efficient as possible. However, if a cellphone's microphone is the easiest piece to

Bottleneck Matrix

Plateau	Common Bottleneck
$500 K	Idle or Confused Staff/Freelancers
$1 M	Founder Beyond Capacity to Manage Everything
$2 M	Not Enough Large Prospects and/or Too Many Small Prospects
$5 M	Quality Control Founder Holding Back Sales/Marketing
$10 M	Losing Proposals or Missing Opportunities Sales/Marketing Team Overwhelm
Any Stage	Flakey Staff Sales Consuming Too Much Time Lack of Talented Staff

build, and the screen the hardest, then the manufacturer will quickly end up with a backlog of microphones if they only focus on efficiency. Microphones will be produced much more quickly than the screens (the bottleneck), but they can't do anything with the excess microphones since they need both items to produce a phone. According to Goldratt, instead of focusing on the efficiency of every step in the manufacturing process, they should focus on fixing the bottlenecks.

Goldratt proposed that instead of running a manufacturing stage 24/7 simply because that provides the lowest cost and the most output they could get from the process, manufacturers should instead focus on producing items only when they are needed. This strategy would introduce the concept of "just in time" manufacturing instead of persistent manufacturing.

Although Goldratt's book focuses on manufacturing, the theory of constraints can be adapted to any business. When attempting to grow yours, there are specific bottlenecks you will face at every key stage of growth, which you will learn throughout this book.

The best part about fixing bottlenecks is that they have a system-wide effect when you fix them. They can ripple through the whole company to improve numerous areas at once. I'll provide plenty of examples as we go along.

Sales Bottleneck

In order to help you develop your own Bottleneck Breakthrough skills, each section of the book covers one of the *6 Growth Levers* and the related bottlenecks that I have helped clients eliminate. As an introduction, here's a great example from the *Marketing Lever* to help you see the power of breaking through bottlenecks.

One of my preferred areas to blow out bottlenecks is the sales process. Closing prospects is the single most important part of every business, but it is typically very inefficient when I review it in real life. You might think it would be more streamlined or use more widely known best practices. But you would be amazed at how much of a mess it is in many companies, even in those doing $100 million a year in revenue.

On the front end of the sales process is the qualification step. Most businesses waste a lot of time here since they don't have any way to filter out unqualified prospects. They end up taking calls from anyone, creating proposals without uncovering their budget, or submitting bids on jobs they have no chance of ever winning. The list of ways to waste energy around closing is long.

Enter the pre-qualification.

For most of my clients, we implement this through a questionnaire on their website, built with a tool named Typeform (*bbg.li/typeform*), requiring all prospects to complete before they go any further in the sales process. I know you might be scared to implement something like this, especially if you're not getting enough quality leads as it is. I get it. When cash flow is tight, anyone with a pulse can seem like the next meal ticket.

But when you put up a filter, those prospects that can afford to use your solution end up appreciating this process and are easier to close. Plus, it weeds out all of the tire kickers that waste your time.

A prospecting questionnaire does not need to be

overwhelming. It just needs to target the key factors that you want your clients to have in order to determine if that prospect is the right one for you. We'll go into more detail on a specific case study using this bottleneck solution in Chapter 4.

On-boarding Bottleneck

One more example bottleneck occurred in a company that offered a great piece of software that helped their small business clients improve their marketing. Amazingly, they were already getting a thousand new subscribers a month on a one dollar trial. The trial went for fourteen days, and then it switched to a $97-a-month subscription.

The software worked extremely well, delivering results for their clients, magically. They approached me to find more affiliates to promote it to scale their growth.

While performing my due diligence, I asked them how long the average person used the program, and was shocked when they said only 2.4 months. This meant the average client value was around $214. Their product should have easily had an average client-lifetime value (CLV) of $600–$700, if not more, based on how effective it was for their clients. We discussed the problem of the low retention and I told them that they didn't need more traffic or leads from affiliates, but instead needed to work on retention levels first.

Like many new software programs, its weakness arose from the fact that it was overwhelming to use. The on-boarding process was horrible, and the user interface was even worse.

While making my pitch to improve their retention, I walked them through an example of another marketing software company (Company B) that had just invested heavily in improving their on-boarding. Company B had struggled with retention for years, but recognized that when new clients actually put the software to use, they stuck around for the long term.

After researching their retention issue, I estimated we could quadruple their profits by simply addressing this bottleneck. Once that was solved, we could move on to recruit more affiliates, attracting them more effectively with the improved CLV.

When I presented the analysis and my recommendations to fix the low retention, I was shocked when they said they weren't interested in working on that. The data was so clear to me, and the benefits, both short and long-term, were massive. Unfortunately, they were fixated on adding more affiliates to pour leads into their leaky bucket. As a result, we parted ways because I knew getting affiliates would be 10 times harder than it needed to be with such a low CLV. I'm not a masochist looking for battles that can't be won.

The punchline to the story is that the company has stagnated over the six years since, stuck at the same plateau, while Company B's improved on-boarding helped them continue growing into the stratosphere in the same timeframe. They even raised $125 million of capital to accelerate that growth.

ACTION ITEMS

Below is a list of the most common bottlenecks I see over and over. There are chapters, or sections of a chapter, in this book devoted to each one. If one jumps out to you as being a major problem right now, read that chapter and get it fixed.

This book was written to walk you through the key leverage points in every business, equipping you along the way to find and fix your bottlenecks. It ends in chapter 13 where you create your own Bottleneck Breakthrough Plan.

My hope is that this book will become your growth manual, and that you will come back to it anytime you need to tackle the next bottleneck in your business.

TRAFFIC PILLARS (CHAPTER 5)

Getting more prospects is the siren song of business owners. Every client comes to me thinking this is their biggest bottleneck, especially when they consume constant hype about the latest and greatest marketing channel (like Facebook ads). Most of the time it is a novel distraction from bigger bottlenecks they should be dealing with.

If you don't have a consistent source of quality leads coming in, you likely have a traffic problem. Developing Traffic Pillars is a key method for scaling revenue and is incredibly powerful when your business is ready for it. The beauty is that most Traffic Pillars can be started small and expanded as your company develops the capability to handle the added lead volume.

STRATEGY (CHAPTERS 2 & 3)

Strategy is a word that is abused and misused regularly. Playing off the definition of *"a plan of action designed to achieve a major aim,"* I try to use it properly with two specific bottlenecks: Big Ideas and Optimization.

The Big Idea helps you differentiate yourself from the competition, makes it easier for prospects to know what they'll get from you, and boosts all of your marketing communications to work more effectively. Look into the Big Idea if you are losing prospects to competitors or you aren't getting a worthwhile response from your current marketing.

CLOSING (CHAPTER 6)

This is my favorite bottleneck to work on because the revenue improvement is almost instant, and there are so many ways to quickly optimize the closing process. Dig into Closing if you aren't winning at least 30% of proposals, your sales team is not hitting quotas, or you're spending significant time just qualifying leads.

MANAGEMENT (CHAPTERS 7 TO 9)

Every business owner hates this topic, equating it to "bureaucracy." This ends up being one of the biggest bottlenecks to significant growth, since each revenue plateau* requires additional management skills to succeed. I've boiled management down to the most effective hacks used by my clients (those running companies <$50 million).

Dig into Management as soon as you can stomach it. It will always be a bottleneck you can improve, whether it involves recruiting better talent or getting the most from your staff. McKinsey, Bain, and BCG are all billion dollar management consulting firms for a reason. You may not know of them, but they silently serve Fortune 500 companies in order to help them keep growing and stay competitive.

---

* Review the Bottleneck Matrix on page 6 if you need a refresher on them.

SYSTEMS (CHAPTER 10)

This is another topic very few business owners enjoy. The result is that they end up operating as a firefighter, filling each day with putting out fires that could have been prevented if systems and checklists existed for their staff to follow. This is another area the Fortune 500 get right by documenting how to fulfill their clients, allowing them to recruit and upgrade their staff any time it is necessary.

One massive bottleneck can show up when your staff finally learns by trial and error how to do their job, but never documents it. They can end up holding you hostage with poor performance or attitude because they know you can't replace them.

Dig into Systems if you have staff you can't fire because of their deep experience and a lack of documentation detailing how they perform their job, or if you're dealing with unprofitable projects or quality control issues. Reinventing the wheel on every new hire or project is a massive opportunity cost holding your company back.

MINDSET (CHAPTER 14)

As the leader of your business, you set the strategy and direction. You also establish the culture and attitude that it develops. If you still find the company stuck at key plateaus even after fixing the bottlenecks above, then looking internally is likely the best bottleneck to tackle.

Dig into Mindset if you are tired of business owners who do not appear to be as talented as you somehow managing to grow more profitable companies, or if you find the same unexplainable issues repeatedly cropping up. I've found that dealing with my bad mental programming has produced the greatest improvement in my consulting (and the rest of my life). That was the biggest bottleneck waiting to be tackled.

Want A Shortcut?

Want a shortcut? Go to *bbg.li/assessment* and take the Bottleneck Breakthrough Assessment. Your answers will go through the Bottleneck Matrix and generate a report with predicted bottlenecks, as well as recommendations on how to remove them.

It is continually being updated as more businesses get results from using it, so my hope is that it will become a useful tool for you any time you need clarity on what to tackle next to unlock more growth.

Get A Boost To Finish The Book

Go to *www.bbg.li/guide* and enter your email to receive a completely customized, action-focused, weekly email from me that adjusts to the pace you're reading through the book.

Strategy

> "A COMPANY CAN OUTPERFORM RIVALS ONLY IF IT CAN
> ESTABLISH A DIFFERENCE THAT IT CAN PRESERVE."
> — *Michael Porter*

Strategy is one of the most misused words in business today, stripping it of its power and significance for business owners. Having worked closely with some of the greatest business strategy minds, starting with Dan Kennedy, then Chet Holmes, Jay Abraham, and Perry Marshall, I have seen firsthand how the right strategy can unlock tremendous growth.

What is strategy, though?

It has two applications in my clients' businesses, and sets the foundation for this section in the *Bottleneck Breakthrough Method.*

1) The effort of establishing a difference that can be preserved
This is commonly referred to as positioning, and can also include business models (how you make money). All activity in the business comes out of this strategy, and it is

usually altered only when responding to major changes in the market or when innovation creates a breakthrough.

2) *The effort of defining and organizing activities to achieve a desired outcome*
This is executional, focusing on achieving a strategic objective that supports the long-term goals of the company. It determines which tactics are used and in which order based on the resources (time, money, and staff) available.

Every business owner I have met struggles with being overwhelmed by executional strategy. There are just too many options to pursue when trying to grow their company. When you add the volume of new software promising to make their project management easier or marketing tools claiming to drive endless leads that are ready to buy, knowing what to pursue and in what order is a chronic need.

Chapter 2 walks you through developing brilliant positioning by finding your Big Idea that cuts through the clutter of the marketplace to draw prospects to you. Chapter 3 shows you how to assess and improve any part of your business, making executional strategy much easier to prioritize.

The Big Idea

"THE BASIC APPROACH TO POSITIONING IS NOT TO
CREATE SOMETHING NEW AND DIFFERENT, BUT TO
MANIPULATE WHAT'S ALREADY IN THE MIND, TO
RE-TIE THE CONNECTIONS THAT ALREADY EXIST."

— *Al Ries & Jack Trout*

A few years ago, I heard Perry Marshall interview the marketing
director of a company that manufactured very large (six-foot
to 20-foot) industrial fans for some very boring applications
in warehouses and livestock yards. The company produced a
great product, but everything about their business was boring.
Even their name was bland: "HVLS Fan Company." HVLS
was the acronym for the types of fans they made, which were
High Volume, Low Speed fans.

Obviously, no farmer is going to get excited about a fan to
cool off their dairy cattle.

After they'd been in business for a few years, they started
catching on when everyone would comment, *"That's a big-ass
fan!"* upon seeing their fans at a trade show. Around that time,

they brought in Bill the marketing guy, and he immediately demanded that they change their name to "Big Ass Fans."

Like any change, everyone in the company fought it. Plus, they are based in Lexington, Kentucky, where using foul language was pretty much taboo in the conservative community.

     All change is resisted, except by the person that came up with the idea.

After a battle of wills, Bill's will and determination eventually won. So, in 2003 the company officially changed their name from HVLS Fan Company to Big Ass Fans. The amount of press and interest that came from it was nothing short of a viral sensation. Bill was interviewed on every edgy morning radio show across the U.S., written up in newspapers, and even interviewed by the BBC because of the shocking new name.

They leveraged the heck out of it and have been growing like gangbusters since. In just the first four years after the name change they grew by 400%, making the first Inc. 5,000 list in 2007, and they have been on it ever since. Unless you have been living under a rock, you would recognize that this growth was sustained through the Great Recession, too.

This is a wonderful example of a Big Idea, which is something that grabs your market's attention and presents a solution in a new and possibly unusual way.

More often than not, Big Ideas center around your product or service, so don't think you need to change your company name right now just because Big Ass Fans did it successfully.

At the end of the day, you want people to remember whatever it is you promise to deliver. And with Big Ass Fans, you will never forget it, even though you'll likely never buy one. In fact, I was at the gym recently, and noticed two huge ceiling fans that had a little logo on the center hub. I'll give you one guess which company it was and the story it instantly reminded me of.

Still Not Convinced?

In case you weren't already aware, every method available to get your message in front of potential prospects is saturated, and everyone is suffering from information overload. Have you looked at a magazine or newspaper lately? I would estimate that most are nearing a 50/50 split between advertisements and editorial (content).

Go online and you can't miss the banner ads, display ads, text ads, pop-up ads, sidebar ads, news feed ads, and retargeting ads all designed to sell you something. There's just no end in sight to the amount of advertisements jumping in front of you, trying to get your attention.

To combat this barrage on their attention, many people have resorted to using tools like ad blockers to reduce the "noise" so they can actually use a website effectively. It's a constant battle between the companies shouting for attention to get prospects to buy their stuff, and the prospects trying to keep from being distracted.

Google recently eliminated the right sidebar of ads. This is the single biggest change to their AdWords platform since it was created in October of 2000. Whole industries were built on those sidebar ads, with companies spending well over $1 million per month on them. And now they have vanished.

Cutting through the noise for your business is more important now than at anytime in modern history. In the case of Google Ads, you simply cannot throw more money at it to get noticed. It has to be of interest to people searching, or else Google won't show your ad, regardless of how much you're willing to pay.

I'm sure your product or service is amazing, but if you want to see how unremarkable your positioning is, just Google your tagline, mission statement, or headline on your website or latest brochure. Put quotation marks around the phrase in Google and you'll see the thousands of websites listing the exact same statement for their product or service. This should help you see that you are just part of the undifferentiated white noise in the world to potential prospects. This means you will be known only by word of mouth until you unlock a Big Idea that will differentiate your company, product, or service.

It Takes Time

You may be tempted to blow off developing a Big Idea because you have enough fires to put out right now, and you're just scavenging for a quick fix to drive some new revenue. Fair enough. Big Ideas are definitely not a quick fix.

A great story of a Big Idea taking time to develop comes from Jack Canfield, co-author of the *Chicken Soup for the Soul* book empire with his partner Mark Victor Hansen. They had decided to work on the book after having countless people ask them at conferences to publish their inspirational stories. They compiled the first 101 stories into a manuscript, then visited publishers in New York, only to be turned down by every single one. Eventually, they were introduced to a small publisher in Florida who loved the book. The problem was that they didn't have a name for it.

So Jack and Mark made it their focus, meditating on it every morning and night. Then one night, Jack went to bed with the intention, *"I will wake up with the perfect book title."* He had a dream in which a hand wrote *"Chicken Soup for the Soul"* on a chalkboard (this was in the early '90s, before whiteboards took over). He woke up with the title in his head, and the rest, as they say, is history. The book went on to sell over 100 million copies worldwide.

With that said, if you decide to wait on developing your Big Idea, I recommend at least finishing this chapter so you can let the concept back-process in your subconscious.

Create Your Big Idea

The best way to accelerate the process of developing a Big Idea is by creating what's known as a value curve, making sure that your idea is unlike that of any of your competitors, while still meeting customer desires. The process is outlined in the book *Blue Ocean Strategy* by W. Chan Kim and Renée Mauborgne. As they demonstrate throughout the book, this process can unlock a *Blue Ocean* of opportunity and get you out of the bloody red ocean of commoditized competition.

In the book, they use a graph like the one on page 25 to visualize the factors an industry competes on, referring to it as the Strategy Canvas. With it, they recommend that you not only look at the factors from competitors but also from alternatives prospects choose from. Alternative industries and markets are a consistent source of ways I've found to differentiate for many businesses.

One famous example is the innovation of the drive-through for fast-food restaurants that is now used millions of times every day. It was originally invented by banks in 1928 with their drive-up tellers. This ingenious concept wasn't adopted by restaurants until 1947, almost two decades later. Then it took McDonald's another 28 years until they added it in 1975. Just think of all the additional revenue the fast-food industry missed out by delaying this feature!

The most important factor to address on the value curve is to uncover the desires of customers, as well as possible non-customers. Sometimes the market for converting non-customers is easier to get to, and possibly larger than the market for existing customers of your competition.

The best example of converting non-customers in *Blue Ocean Strategy* is [yellow tail], which is made by Casella Wines. They felt the market of wine drinkers had become saturated, competing on factors that were complex and seemingly arbitrary. So they looked to the much larger market of beer and cocktail drinkers to see what it would take to convert them to drink their wine.

Looking at the Strategy Canvas for [yellow tail], you can see the factors the wine industry competed on and the related value curves of premium and budget wines. Instead of trying to go head-to-head with either end of the market, Casella went through the process Kim and Mauborgne define as the

Four Actions Framework*, which asks the following questions:

1. What are the factors in your industry that are taken for granted and should be **eliminated?**
2. What factors should be **reduced** well below the industry's standard?
3. What factors should be **raised** well above the industry's standard?
4. What are new factors that should be **created** that the industry has never offered?

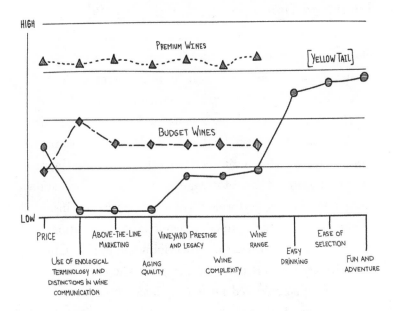

THE STRATEGY CANVAS OF [YELLOW TAIL]

---

* © Kim and Mauborgne, *Blue Ocean Strategy,* page 29.

By looking at the beer and cocktail non-customers, they saw the factors of easy drinking, ease of selection, and fun and adventure as the priorities and **added** them to their value curve. Not only did they convert huge numbers of people in a much larger market, but their market redefinition also reduced the complexity of production, lowering their overhead. Casella used all four actions to unlock an uncontested *Blue Ocean* market.

In the process of creating a new value curve and using the Four Actions Framework, I have yet to walk away empty-handed. It produces at least one differentiator that is worth testing to see how prospects respond to it, and it typically leads to more useful insights.

Lions and Tigers and Gymnasts, Oh My!

There are a number of fantastic case studies outlined in *Blue Ocean Strategy*. If you are a reader like me, you will want to have a copy of the book because it is an invaluable resource that you will revisit throughout the rest of your entrepreneurial career.

My favorite case study in the book was from Cirque du Soleil.

You may not be aware, but Cirque du Soleil's direct competition is actually Ringling Brothers and other three-ring circuses. They both featured feats of strength and physical coordination incapable of being performed by mere mortals. But instead of competing on the distinctive characteristics that Ringling Brothers had established since their founding in 1884, Cirque du Soleil used the Four Actions Framework to develop a new value curve that unlocked a new *Blue Ocean* in the process.

When you look at the business model of the conventional circus, you will see that they have been in a downward spiral since the late '90s. Their costs have continued to rise, but increasing ticket prices in order to remain competitive was problematic. Just think of the expense of hauling tigers and elephants across the country. Plus, they cater to kids, so the tickets have always been family budget-friendly.

In less than 20 years since the industry decline started, Ringling Brothers finally had to close after 146 years in business.

The first thing you notice about Cirque du Soleil is that they started with the first question of the Four Action Framework and *eliminated* the animals from their show. That's an impressive cut to overhead. The stars of the show became the gymnasts who once performed the trapeze, tightrope, and other acrobatic feats. The gymnasts were much easier to source and maintain than tigers. And the last time I checked, the salary for a gymnast is much lower than that of the team it takes to keep a tiger alive (and keep it from eating everyone else).

The quality of the venue was then *raised* to a comfortable theatre-style setting. No more bench seats in an arena or under a big tent. Paired with their *creation* of themes and artistic direction, this made it more appealing to the non-customer, those who might traditionally attend the philharmonic or sports games to entertain for business. These improvements attracted a higher-end client and allowed them to justify a higher ticket price. With their prices ranging from $60 to $200 and more, Cirque du Soleil has unlocked a business that entrepreneurial dreams are made of.

Big Idea Fuel

You should be convinced by now that a Big Idea is necessary

for real, sustainable growth. You may not need it to get past your current plateau, but you will need it if you want to keep growing for years to come, just like Big Ass Fans and Cirque du Soleil.

So what should you be doing while you are waiting for your Big Idea to materialize?

Testimonials! They are the fuel to help materialize your Big Idea. You will see the unique factors your clients care about that you can use to hone your value curve and create your Big Idea, just like Big Ass Fans did. Plus, they help all marketing and sales efforts perform better.

Since you have been in business for a while, you have sources for these testimonials just waiting to be written. Begin collecting as many as possible from past endorsements, written reviews, case studies, or actual testimonials from past clients.

A car dealer I know has pictures of every person who has ever bought a car from him. He plastered them all over his cubicle and then started building a binder filled with the pictures. He would show the pictures to prospects so they could see the multiple generations of families that had purchased cars from him. The photo album was visual proof of his success, leveraging social proof* and making the new customer more comfortable since so many others like them had benefitted from doing business with him over the years.

If you sell something physical, like cars, homes, or jewelry,

---

* The persuasion mechanism made famous by professor Robert Cialdini in his book *Influence*. It relies on humans to look for ways to shortcut decision making, and assumes that if someone else like them did something, then it should be good for them to do it, too.

getting photos with customers is a breeze. Simply ask them if you can take their picture to add to your album of happy customers. If you serve a local area, reviews on sites like Yelp, Google My Business, and Facebook are powerful because they can show up in Google when a prospect is researching you online. Putting photos of your clients on your website is useful, too.

Jay Abraham, the godfather of modern business strategy, did this over the past few decades, and he ended up with a 400-page book. It is an eight-by-ten book containing the letters of endorsement he has received over the years. Reviewing it while I was sitting in his office was just another contributing factor in building his credibility, especially in light of the fact that some of the letters are from the titans of industry, like a key executive at FedEx.

Do It For Them

The single biggest factor holding you back from getting testimonials is simply how difficult it is for your clients to write something worthwhile. It's not because they don't love working with you, it's just that they don't always know what to say.

Here are my favorite methods to solve this problem.

The first, and most tactful, approach is to offer to write the testimonial for them. When it is completed, you can email or mail it to them for a final edit. Every time I have done this my clients have thanked me for it, since they weren't sure how to go about writing it, and I saved them some valuable time.

You might also write several optional testimonials as examples for your customers.

A friend of mine is a real estate broker whose team works with buyers, sellers, and investors. He has several template endorsements for each of these three segments that he sends as an email at the end of escrow, with some links to his Trulia, Zillow, Google My Business, Facebook, and Yelp profiles. His clients get the hint and appreciate the time-saving templates, and their testimonials strengthen his profiles.

Finally, another method I have used is to interview my clients, recording them (with their permission), and using their answers to craft the testimonial for them to approve. When I owned a mortgage brokerage, we created a testimonial CD that was a compilation of the best endorsements about our services and included it in our welcome package to prospects.

ACTION STEPS

If you don't have a Big Idea yet, do the following:

1. Draw out your value curve. Evaluate what your competitors' value curves might be, too. Put them on the Strategy Canvas to compare against. I suggest a whiteboard or online at *bbg.li/strategy-canvas*.
2. Add the value curve of an alternative solution, like beer and cocktail drinkers for [yellow tail].
3. Look at the competing factors and go through the Four Actions Framework to find what to *eliminate*, *reduce*, *raise*, and *create*.
4. Work with your team to start developing your Big Idea into a clearly defined sentence. You may have go through this a few times until it hits the bulls-eye.

If you don't have a robust testimonials library, start collecting them now.

1. Pick 10 happy clients to ask to give testimonials. Even if only 2 or 3 give you one, they will provide a big boost to your sales and marketing efforts.
2. Interview the happy clients if you want to get powerful insights that will help drive your Big Idea development.
3. Save the testimonials in a Google Doc or somewhere easy for everyone on your team to reference.
4. For extra credit, get pictures and videos with each testimonial. Phones are great to capture these when you're with clients.

CHAPTER 3

Optimization

"THAT WHICH IS MEASURED IMPROVES.
THAT WHICH IS MEASURED AND REPORTED
IMPROVES EXPONENTIALLY."

— *Karl Pearson*

There is a great story about a new bride making a hearty dinner for her husband, trying her best to be a star homemaker. She knew her father had loved the glazed ham her mother made, and it was a big hit at holidays with her extended family. As she was preparing it, she was confused about one step in the recipe where it required her to cut off both ends of the ham, so she gave her mom a quick call for directions.

She asked her how much to cut off at both ends, and in the middle of asking, she wondered why cut them off at all? Her mother said she didn't know, telling her that was the way her mother always did it. So her mom called Grandma to ask.

Mom asked Grandma why she cut off the ends of the ham, and Grandma just started chuckling. Once she regained her composure, she replied, *"I only did that because the ham wouldn't fit in the pan I had!"*

Tradition can obviously be a great thing, passing what works from generation to generation, especially when it is associated with heartwarming family memories. There are also traditions that no longer make sense, just like cutting the ends off the ham when the oven and pan are much larger than the ones your grandmother used 50-plus years ago.

Your business may not have traditions, but it definitely has processes that were put in place for a different time and with different resources. Some of them are benign, like cutting the ends off the ham. There are others that may not be malignant, but they are clearly bottlenecks that need to be updated and improved.

This whole book is intended to help you find and fix those bottlenecks anytime you want. The first step in mastering this process is to make sure your mindset is properly focused.

Continuous Improvement

Once a business hits the proverbial comfort level of the owner, it will shift away from growth and into a state of maintenance. During this transition, the culture will shift as new staff who are attracted to maintaining the company are brought in. When the company was growing, the employees that thrived were the ones who could handle uncertainty and were comfortable with changing objectives and roles, sometimes on a week-by-week basis.

When structure and certainty develop in an organization as a byproduct of learning what works and repeating it efficiently to meet demand, the employees that helped grow the company start leaving. The routine is boring to them, and everything feels like it takes ten times longer to execute compared to the company's early, growth-oriented days.

This pattern happens to every company at some point, regardless of size. With this change, the skill of challenging assumptions and finding ways to improve things disappears across the company. It's inevitable and is just part of the business life cycle.

Publicly traded companies try to revive the growth culture by bringing in a new CEO. However, most of the time they're just bringing in a manager of the status quo who uses some different buzzwords than the last one did. Just look at what Yahoo! experienced over the past four years when they tried this with ex-Google exec Marissa Mayer.

Every once in awhile a Lee Iacocca or Jack Welch will show up and provide the energy and vision to reset the culture to stimulate new growth.

Instead of trying to roll the dice on hiring a new CEO to replace you in your company, I think that adopting the mindset of continuous improvement is the single best chance you have at growing or streamlining your business to its fullest potential. The Japanese call this "Kaizen," and it became wildly famous in the late 1980's.

It means "Good Change," and its core philosophy is that *"big results come from many small changes accumulated over time."*

The Bottleneck Breakthrough Method definitely aligns with this philosophy. The cornerstone of the method is to always be on the lookout for better and easier ways to do what you're already doing.

Challenging Assumptions

Dave Greeley, a great friend of mine, has imparted many valuable insights to me over the years, which is no surprise given the successful career he had as a Creative Director for the global ad agency, BBDO Worldwide. The one he shared that serves you best right now is to always challenge assumptions. For example, why did the new wife cut off the ends of the ham, and did that action still serve her needs today?

Identifying assumptions is difficult, as most actions are carried out on autopilot or in a reactive mode. Einstein saw this, and said, *"We cannot solve our problems with the same thinking we used when we created them."*

Thankfully, Dave shared the method to help find assumptions that I use consistently with my clients and in my own business. It's called "Zero Based Thinking."

ZBT is best started by asking the following question:

"With what I know today about past situations like this one, and the way I dealt with them, would I want to do the same thing again this time?"

You can only answer *"Yes"* or *"No,"* giving you great clarity on what your options are.

If the answer is yes, then you can keep doing what's already working. If the answer is no, then you can decide to stop it or restructure it to make it ideal for today. *

ZBT helps cut through all the clutter and emotion that the situation carries with it today. It acts like a blank slate to

---

* We'll dig into ways to confront restructuring relationships in Chapter 9, as well as how to better clarify what you really want from your business in Chapter 12.

start over and rebuild something as well as possible, given the current knowledge, skills, and resources available to you.

Here's a recent situation I encountered with Ecela Spanish, a client with amazing Spanish immersion programs in South America. Our goal was to develop the marketing and sales plan for one of their niche programs.

They work with many students who come to their program with financial aid needs. They present students with custom options such as flexible payment arrangements to make it as feasible as possible. As I was looking at the effort they expended to collect payments by creating a nearly custom payment plan and follow-up process for each student, I started with the ZBT question above.

The answer was no, they wouldn't start with the custom payment plan. As I investigated their processes further, I found that student enrollment varied from six weeks to ten months before they attended a program. Because of this timeline variability, Ecela had formed the assumption that they needed to customize the payment options for each student to make it as feasible as possible for them to attend.

We concluded that a possible improvement was to offer more structured payment plans, which could streamline cash flow and reduce collection efforts. We tested out a simple plan, giving students two options when they enrolled. One option was a monthly payment plan over eight months, and the other was a more traditional option of paying the tuition all at once, no later than six weeks before they were to start their course. The first round of testing showed that 40 percent of the new students chose the monthly payment plan, while another 10 percent chose the single payment option. The remaining 50 percent requested a custom plan, just as the company had offered in the past.

Having 40 percent of new students choose the payment plan will stabilize Ecela's cash flow for this program, reducing the seasonal spikes that occurred every spring and summer when the courses are all running. The changes also resulted in 50 percent less staff effort to coordinate and collect payment. Since this is just the first iteration of this new approach, I'm confident we can continue to improve these numbers, streamlining the process and cash flow significantly as we grow their Spanish immersion programs.

Once you start challenging assumptions, you'll need one more foundational component to build upon as you implement the *Bottleneck Breakthrough Method* in your business.

Measurement

Pearson's Law is a quote by Karl Pearson, the 19th century mathematician who is said to have developed modern statistics, that I used below the title of this chapter. It is one of my all time favorite pieces of business wisdom.

"That which is measured improves. That which is measured and reported improves exponentially."

With the advances in technology that allow us to track so many activities in our business, effective measurement simply requires choosing to do it and then finding the key activities to measure its effectiveness.

Ron Johnson built quite a resume, helping expand Target's merchandising and then leading the Apple Store to great success for the computer giant. In late 2011 he was hired as the new CEO of J.C. Penney to try revitalizing the 111-year-old retailer.

Johnson started with massive changes, eliminating all discounts by moving to a fixed pricing matrix, and then changed their marketing strategies to attract a higher-end clientele. His biggest mistake was to roll them all out at once, nationwide.

The results were disastrous. Johnson spent $1 billion in capital over his 17 month tenure, reducing Penney's reserves from $1.8 billion down to $930 million. Revenue dropped by 25 percent in 2012, resulting in a $1 billion loss, and their market value dropped by 50 percent.

Johnson was famous for ignoring data from market research, and he felt he only needed to follow his gut instinct to turn the company around. He even ignored veteran staff that encouraged him to test his ideas out in a few stores to validate its effectiveness before taking on the risk of rolling them out further.

Avinash Kaushik is a leader in the world of data and analytics who coined the label "HiPPO" back in 2006 when describing leaders like Johnson. It stands for "Highest Paid Person's Opinion," and characterizes this type of individual as being so self-assured that they don't need others' ideas or data to validate their instincts.

Needless to say, leading by gut feeling and ignoring data is as risky as it gets. Plus, it creates an environment where everyone stops sharing ideas because they are never heard or acknowledged.*

---

* Yes, even you need to rely on data, Mr. "I'm the next Steve Jobs".

What To Measure

Every business has two or three key activities that are crucial to its success. When these activities are measured as a number or percentage, they are called Key Performance Indicators. By monitoring them on a regular basis, you can see trends develop and can then make changes.

Every business type and industry has a common set of KPIs that are useful for most of the companies in it. For professional service companies, the KPIs could be utilization rate, contracted revenue, or profit. KPIs for SaaS companies are churn, monthly recurring revenue, and customer acquisition cost.

The most fundamental KPI for any business is profit on a cash basis. Cash is the lifeblood of every business, so knowing how much more comes in than goes out every month is the ultimate indicator of health (or failure).

As you dig into various KPIs for your business, you will inevitably go down numerous rabbit holes, finding activities you can track in every part of your business that are useful indicators. My suggestion is to start small and track one or two activities that are crucial to your business's success. Once you have a tracking and reporting process in place that you can trust to be accurate, then you can expand and add other metrics to review.

There's nothing worse than seeing a half-implemented data capture and reporting system, so focus on making it useful before making it comprehensive.

How To Measure

As with most technology available to businesses today, the options are nearly endless, and you can become overwhelmed with those choices. The resource section on the website is ever-expanding and frequently updated, so utilize it as you evaluate your options for tracking and reporting on KPIs in your business.

Here is a short list of tools I recommend to every client, regardless of their business model or industry.

GOOGLE ANALYTICS + TAG MANAGER

The world of website analytics is as complex as any specialized discipline today. Regardless of the hype behind any one, there is no perfect tool that will be able to track every unique visitor across every device they have and every action they take on your website. With that said, Google Analytics (*bbg.li/analytics*) is free and is reliable enough to make well-educated decisions from. It can do today what expensive analytics suites could do ten years ago, but it doesn't require the $20,000+ per year license fee and additional $10,000+ configuration investment.

You can deploy Analytics in its basic version by just putting the script in the header of every page on your website, and you'll get sufficient functionality out of it right from the start.

If you have a more complex website, whether as a SaaS app, e-commerce, or other function that involves more than just clicking between basic PHP or HTML pages, then I would recommend using Google's new Tag Manager tool to set up Analytics through. Initially, it is challenging to configure for more websites, but there are enough agency and freelance providers available now to handle it for you. It's easy to overpay for initial software setups, but as a ballpark figure, KPI's configured in Google Tag Manager should be under $500.

HOTJAR

While we are covering website-based tracking tools, I always recommend the visitor tracking tool Hotjar (*bbg.li/hotjar*). It's a new player in the space and hasn't raised prices to enterprise levels yet, so it's a great option for any budget. You can record mouse movement of visitors to see what they click and scroll to, as well as create heat maps of each page on your site to see what people click on and scroll to cumulatively. You can also deploy polls on any page on your site to collect feedback directly from visitors, often generating useful insights in the process.

Hotjar is a great tool built for testing and optimizing changes on your website. It is invaluable for companies that rely on their website for a large part of their sales funnel or customer fulfillment process.

XERO

Most businesses under $10 million in annual revenue typically rely on Quickbooks for their bookkeeping needs. Xero (*bbg.li/xero*) is an alternative that I recommend instead, as it is less clunky online compared to Quickbooks, and has more features that don't require additional fees, such as payroll processing in many states in the U.S.

Regardless of what bookkeeping software you choose, keeping it up to date with everything financial is the key. A monthly income statement (or profit & loss statement) based on cash (not accruals) is, in my opinion, the foundation of all KPIs.

SPREADSHEETS

At the end of the day, any tracking tool can export raw data from its database into CSV files that are easy to put into a spreadsheet. Pull data from a few different tools, and you can compile it into a single spreadsheet that is as powerful as the most expensive dashboard tools available.

It may feel like a throwback to use spreadsheets, but exporting data and organizing it doesn't take much time once you get the process sorted out. Plus, you can always tweak it to better fit your needs, much more easily than you can edit many dashboards and fancy reporting software.

Don't get me wrong, I'm a huge fan of data automation and display, but I also know that spreadsheets work every time. In the end, my favorite tool is whichever one gets used and best influences decisions because of it.

ACTION STEPS

Zero Based Thinking and the mindset of continuous improvement work together as the foundation to help you find and fix your bottlenecks.

While you're developing those skills, make sure you have tracking in place to measure and report on your Key Performance Indicators.

1. Is your bookkeeping updated and accurate so you can review your Income Statement monthly? If not, start there.

2. Do you have Google Analytics installed on your website? It takes minutes to set up and collects data forever, so get it configured now.

3. Do a Google search for "KPIs in [inser your industry]" and see what two or three results keep showing up. Figure out how to track them and get it configured.

Once you have tracking in place, get your reporting set up to review your KPIs at least monthly.

1. Review your Income Statement every month to see how profitable you really are, and to stay on top of expenses. Here's a great guide on how to review your Income Statement *bbg.li/income-report*.

2. Review your website traffic every month to see how your marketing efforts are driving results (or not). Here's another great guide on how to create and review your Analytics reports *bbg.li/analytics-report*.

3. Review your other industry specific KPI reports monthly.

LEVER #2

Marketing

"BECAUSE THE PURPOSE OF BUSINESS IS TO CREATE A
CUSTOMER, THE BUSINESS ENTERPRISE HAS TWO—AND ONLY
TWO—BASIC FUNCTIONS: MARKETING AND INNOVATION.
MARKETING AND INNOVATION PRODUCE RESULTS; ALL THE
REST ARE COSTS. MARKETING IS THE DISTINGUISHING,
UNIQUE FUNCTION OF THE BUSINESS."

— *Peter Drucker*

Marketing is the most misunderstood, abused, and ignored part of small businesses today. The speed at which technology is changing how we interact with the world creates more overwhelm for business owners than at any other point in history. Unfortunately, this speed of change leads to costly ignorance for owners, as well as the vendors that sell them marketing solutions.

Without marketing, there simply is no business.

Let's start by breaking marketing down to its most simple definition:

> *Communication aimed at persuading*
> *someone to take a desired action.*

You might think that defines sales, not marketing. You're close, as sales is a component of marketing. Anything you say, do, create, post, print, send, or otherwise communicate to someone to get them to give you money is marketing.

The challenge is to figure out which communications are most effective for your business right now, given your time, money, staffing, industry, and target market, so you can generate growth again.

First, define your funnel. This is the process in which future customers find and purchase something from you. Then dig into the two main levers within that funnel, using Traffic Pillars and Closing to uncover what bottlenecks you can break through.

CHAPTER 4

Your Funnel

"IF YOU CAN'T DESCRIBE WHAT YOU ARE
DOING AS A PROCESS, YOU DON'T KNOW
WHAT YOU ARE DOING."

— *W. Edwards Deming*

I am not a symphony buff, but it doesn't take a genius to know that Joshua Bell is one of the greatest violinists in the world. He packs symphony halls everywhere he goes. He plays a violin that was made in 1713 by Stradivari, and that is now worth $3.5 million.

In 2007 he was on a tour through Washington, D.C. when he was approached by a journalist to try a social experiment, in which he was asked to play as a busker in a Metro station. A few weeks before the experiment took place, he filled the Library of Congress near the station for a free concert. Surely he must have expected to be mobbed while he played, as more than a thousand people would pass him on their way to work.

Not only did he play his Stradivari, but he played what many consider the most difficult violin piece of all time, Bach's "Chaconne," written in 1720. The only difference between his concert performance and this one in the Metro station was his attire. In the Metro station he wore street clothes, just like other buskers, and looked to all the world like an unemployed musician.

He played for forty-three minutes straight, and of the 1,097 people who passed by him, only two people stopped to listen to him. Only twenty-seven people stopped long enough to drop money in his violin case. He raised a whopping thirty-two dollars and change for what was no doubt a jaw-dropping performance.

The experiment ended up earning the journalist a Pulitzer Prize for the story. And I'm going to use it to help you become a better marketer than 95 percent of business owners today.

Think about the details of this story for a minute before we move on. Someone who played before royalty, made as much as $1,000 per minute, and mesmerized audiences around the world was completely ignored without the proper recipe of influence in place . . . also known as MARKETING!

Fundamentals

Hoping to not get too heavy on theory, I want to first establish some fundamentals that are important for you to understand when it comes to effective marketing. The first is taught to every university marketing student. It is referred to as the AIDA framework, and all marketing communication should adhere to it.

Notice that it all starts with attention. Without attention, you end up like Joshua Bell, simply ignored.

Once you capture your audience's attention, you need to create interest, and then desire.

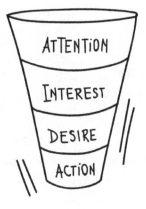

AIDA FUNNEL

ATTENTION

INTEREST

DESIRE

ACTION

Bell never got the chance to create interest or desire because he was lost in the noise of the daily commute. Out of 1,097 people, there were two who stopped and listened as long as they could. One was a fan that recognized him (already aware and interested), while the other was an ex-violin player who had an ear for the quality of Bell's performance.

Finally, you need to get your audience to take an action. In most cases, this is simply to purchase something from you.

In Bell's case, since people could pay what they wanted, he managed to get twenty-seven people to contribute something for his effort. Taking out the five dollars paid by the ex-violinist, he netted twenty-seven dollars from twenty-six people. Just over one dollar each, which is about what a homeless panhandler would get if he was just sitting there asking for donations.

Needless to say, Bell's experiment helped show that without the pieces of the AIDA framework in place, you won't get paid anywhere close to what your products or services are truly worth. And it disproves the old myth from *Field of Dreams* that so many business owners mistakenly believe, that *"If you build it, they will come."*

Know Your Funnel

If you keep up with marketing trends, you're no doubt familiar with the topic of "funnels," which has become a buzzword since early 2013. There are countless marketing tools aimed at helping you improve your funnel, from landing page tools and email auto-responders to analytics tracking and full-blown marketing automation suites that cost more than your car. In addition to the tools, there are now funnel agencies, seminars, certification courses, training programs, podcasts, and coaching. All of them are ready to serve you and charge you a princely sum, but the majority of them have no track record or performance guarantee.

The reality is that funnels have existed since the dawn of commerce. They have just come into vogue right now because of two factors.

First, the cheap flow of prospects from once-new channels like Google AdWords and search engine results (SEO) has become more costly. Like any medium, competition causes an efficient market to be created around it, raising the price for everyone until only the most profitable (or wasteful) are left to use it. So, having a more efficient marketing funnel is necessary to compete in those channels now.

Second, the capabilities of the Internet and the software running on it continue to grow exponentially. The free version of Google Analytics available today can do more than enterprise-level analytics solutions that were priced at $20,000 per year just a decade ago.

To clarify, a funnel is simply the steps you take a prospect through to make them a customer. Every business has one. You just need to define yours so you know how to improve it if you've never paid attention to it.

Going back to the AIDA graphic, I'll bet you noticed that it is shaped like a funnel. That funnel graphic has been around since the early 1960's, and the framework has existed since 1898 (yes, more than 100 years ago).

Again, this stuff isn't new. But it's vital to get it right.

Funnel Stages

When we look at the entire funnel, we see there are three parts that create revenue for every business: generating leads, closing them, and then fulfilling them as clients.

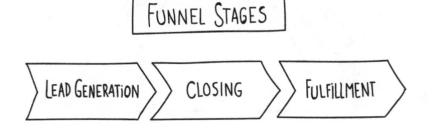

LEAD GEN

As outlined above, the beginning of any funnel starts with *Attention.* Every potential customer in every market is exposed to over 30,000 ads each day. Your job is to create a way to cut through that noise and be noticed. This is easier said than done, as you're well aware.

The best framework I've found to consistently capture attention and generate qualified leads is Message-Market-Media. I learned this from the famed copywriter and author, Dan Kennedy.

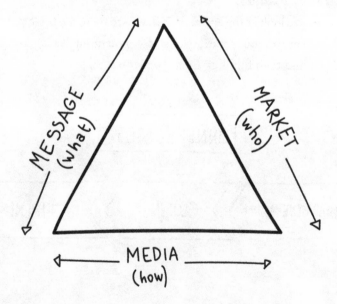

Message: What are you saying?

Marketers define this as your copy, which is the communications used to persuade prospects.

Back to Joshua Bell, he was relying on his music to do the communication. This is the classic mistake that most business owners make; they think that just because they deliver a great product or service, people will tell others about it. It may happen, but it is unlikely to cause fast growth. You can pull out the extreme cases to build your argument around, like Cheesecake Factory*, but it is much easier to create demand by learning how to tell others how well your product or service meets their needs.

Let's start building your message off your Big Idea from Chapter 2.

Market: Who are you speaking to?

Marketers define this as your customer avatar, or profile. These are the details defining who you want to attract to buy your product.

As with most experiments, researchers would be quick to dismiss the commuters as people uninterested in classical violin music. They may not all be Bach or Beethoven buffs, but this particular metro station was used by people of all ranks in the federal government, from a lawyer for the U.S. Postal Service to a consultant for the Department of Transportation, to an IT specialist at the Department of Housing and Urban Development. They may not have forked over $100 for decent seats at

---

* A restaurant with such an amazing and affordable menu that they've never had to advertise to generate customers. The food is so good that everyone comes back for more and tells their friends and family about it.

one of his concerts, but they were sophisticated enough to be able to recognize impressive classical music.

You probably have an idea of who your ideal customer type is by now. If not, this is a must-do. Use the guide at *bbg.li/profile* to develop your ideal customer type.

TIP: A great shortcut to growth is to pursue higher-quality clients. It doesn't require rebranding or retooling your entire business to get them either. Just a willingness to intentionally go after them and even be willing to say "no" to future prospects that might prevent you from being able to serve the larger clients.

Media: How are they receiving the message?

This is the means of delivery. Whether delivered in person, over the phone, printed and mailed, broadcast on TV or radio, put online somewhere, or any of the seemingly countless options available today, it is where most of the marketing activity exists because there are always new media being developed. Plus, there are sales reps and training programs tied to so many media, so business owners fall for the silver-bullet promise that comes with each one.

In Bell's case, the medium was in person in a Metro station. Definitely far from ideal. The complexity of the Message-Market-Media framework is that it works more like a recipe than a checklist. Your goal is to get all three right in any marketing campaign. When you do, it works almost like magic, driving in clients unlike anything you've ever experienced before. But it doesn't guarantee that you can just swap pieces around and keep getting the same results.

So many businesses try to keep two pieces in place (most commonly done with message and market), and expect it to work with any option for the third piece (most commonly swapped with media). Just because the combination of peanut butter and jelly works great on wheat bread, it doesn't necessarily mean it will work as well on sourdough or cheese biscuits.

Messing With The Recipe

A great example of this is a company with a direct mail campaign that generates great leads that wants to try something online. Their campaign consists of a simple postcard (*medium*) that makes an offer for a free consultation (*message*), allowing the prospect to call their office or fill out a consultation request form on their website. The company has a list broker who has found a great list (*market*) that responds to their offer, getting them qualified appointments with prospects at an average cost of $120/each. They close 20 percent of the leads that come in, at a total cost of $600/each ($120 / 20 percent), which is very profitable since their average sale is $4,000.

They decide to try out Facebook ads, uploading their past client email list to let Facebook find more people just like them (through Custom and Lookalike Audiences). They make an ad with the same image on the postcard, along with the copy, and send people to the same web page with the consultation request form. But it doesn't work. They get clicks, and Facebook charges them for each one, but after 1,000 people click through at a cost of $1.25 per click, not a single one fills out the form.

This doesn't mean that Facebook can't work for them, just that they need to figure out if their targeting filters need to be changed (*market*) and then adjust their offer on the landing page (*message*), since it's obviously not working.

It's a great example of creating a peanut butter and jelly sandwich on cheese biscuits.

We will tackle developing the right recipe for your business in the next chapter on traffic, which is all about generating qualified prospects in a controllable and scalable method.

CLOSING SALES

The next stage in the funnel after generating a lead is to determine the prospect's needs and solve them if you are the best provider to do that. We all know this step as "closing the sale" and it is the most neglected part of the funnel that I see in businesses of all sizes.

Most clients I work with have little to no structure to their closing process. This often causes the owner or sales staff to follow the prospect's lead, fielding whatever question they throw at you. Or they end up winging it, reinventing the wheel every time and getting inconsistent results. Or worst of all, they end up turning into an order taker, only providing pricing and terms without any effort to qualify or persuade the prospect.

Yes, persuasion is needed and even welcomed by prospects.

PREQUALIFYING

One of the biggest levers in the sales process is to prequalify leads before spending any time with them. A great case study on the power of prequalifying is from the Mountain Training School, which is a four-year, intensive mountain-guide training program. Like a high quality university, it requires a significant investment, and the interest in it is very strong.

With such a specialized market, every interested student had a mountain of unique personal questions based on their individual situation. The founder would personally handle every inquiry, acting as the de facto admissions department.

Each prospective student would fill out a short questionnaire and then get up to a half-hour call from the founder to discuss their specific issues. This would eat up twenty-plus hours a week. The number of potential students who were actually qualified, could cover the cost, and make the commitment was low, in the 5 percent range.

To improve the system, I looked at how we could improve the quality of leads as well as the quality of the discussions. We looked at follow-through as well as how to improve the on-boarding process so that more students actually paid and committed to the program. The school only wanted to take on twenty-four new students a year at that time because it was the sweet spot for profitability and logistics.

To help them remove this bottleneck, we made the application process much more formal, similar to an application to a traditional university. We added a fee for the application. The questionnaire was expanded to approximately sixty questions, many of which were open-ended, making it much more time-consuming to complete. This new forced-compliance application helped weed out students who were not committed to the process. This was very similar to the red velvet rope technique used at exclusive venues where people line up and wait with anticipation to get in.

Since we were using Typeform (*bbg.li/typeform*) for the application, we were able to include some conditional logic in it. This meant that based on the answers to certain questions, applicants that answered in a way that demonstrated they were highly qualified, would automatically get access to the founder's calendar (using *bbg.li/calendly*) to schedule a more thorough application interview call.

If the questionnaire analysis did not highlight a potential student for the program, the student would get a message saying, *"We'll follow up with you"* after submission. Later, an email would be sent to the potential student stating that, *"It doesn't appear to be the right fit right now. Feel free to reach out in the future if your experience changes."*

At the end of the new application interview calls, the founder would know with certainty who was a worthy applicant and who wasn't, allowing him to grant acceptances on the spot.

In the end, this automation ensured that the founder's time wasn't wasted on potential students who were not appropriate for the program.

These improvements saved the founder approximately twenty hours a week in calls. It also improved his close rate from 12.5 percent to just over 80 percent.*

---

* Over the next few months, we tackled two additional bottlenecks (a Traffic Pillar and a pricing adjustment), which resulted in 324 percent revenue growth over the following two years (70.7 percent in year 1 and 90.3 percent in year 2).

NURTURING

An offshoot of the funnel is the holding pen, where you put everyone that doesn't buy from you. I call this the Lead Incubator, as it allows you to nurture and care for them over time until they mature to a point that it makes sense for them to buy from you. Their decision not to purchase from you yet could be due to any number of reasons, such as timing, trust building, budget, prior obligations with other vendors, etc.

The reason doesn't really matter at this stage. You just need a place for them to be captured so you can communicate with them and keep them from falling through the cracks.

All Customer Relationship Management (CRM) systems are capable of segmenting leads into this bucket. So it's simply a matter of placing them in it after they decide not to purchase from you right now. You can get fancy with how the system organizes them and what communications you send to them over time by segment. But for now, just make sure they're captured and stored somewhere accessible, even if it's just in a spreadsheet somewhere. There's a gold mine in unconverted leads for most businesses.

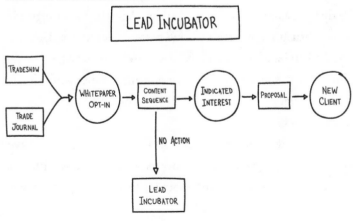

Don't worry about where your company is on this spectrum yet, as we'll dig into it in more depth in a couple chapters on Closing. The key is that you just want to write out your closing process so you have something to review and use as a baseline for improvement.

If you have multiple client segments, be sure to write out the closing process for each one so you can review it later to determine which one offers the most upside to any improvement efforts.

FULFILLMENT

If you've been in business for more than a year, I'm guessing that your client fulfillment process is operating at a satisfactory level. You deliver the product or service with sufficient quality that the client is happy enough with it. This may seem obvious to point out, since no business survives very long without delivering a quality product, but it's important to be aware of the steps in your fulfillment process as you review ways to dramatically grow your business.

You may have fulfilled thousands and thousands of clients by this stage in your business. You can likely do it as effortlessly as you brush your teeth or drive to work every day. This is a blessing and a curse when it comes to writing out what you do. You know the process cold, but it also means that you're likely to miss certain steps when writing it out because your brain fills in the gaps for you.

This is also the reason that so many of my clients have such obvious and simple improvements to make with fulfillment. They stopped thinking about it a long time ago, once they mastered it in its current format.

Yamabe & Horn Engineering had been in business for over thirty years, successfully servicing local municipalities and developers. The senior engineers had completed so many projects that they could instantly visualize every step a new project would require, mentally mapping out the entire project over the next six to nine months. They were so skilled at delivering great projects that the volume of change requests from the contractors building out their plans was well below industry averages. They saw ahead and handled potential problems before they ever happened.

Their challenge came when they were going through significant expansion after we optimized their closing process (outlined in Chapter 6) and they gained new engineers and support staff that weren't as experienced. This caused them to start missing things and having to redesign parts of projects late in the process, which is very costly. Their deep experience had become a weakness as they grew, with all the knowledge locked up in the heads of the senior engineers. The solution was to actually define their project kickoff process and how projects would be planned in a team environment so everyone would be on the same page.

Having an outsider involved (me) to draw out their entire process and document it was a necessity. Regardless of how hard the senior engineers tried to write it all out, they didn't realize how many steps they missed in the documentation process. Any one of those missing steps would have been ruinous for a less experienced team member not to have in their design process.

Your client fulfillment process may not be as complex as a civil engineering firm that builds roads and waterways, but

I guarantee there are many benefits to writing it out. Like everything else in this book, it will help you improve upon your process, making it more efficient and effective over time. Another bonus of documenting it is that you will be able to better set the expectations of your new clients, making them more secure in their decision to purchase from you. By showing them all the steps you take to serve them, you put them at ease, knowing that you're working hard on their behalf.

ACTION STEPS

Draw your funnel. Every single step.

You can get fancy and use software like Lucidchart.com, or you can do what I do and just grab a piece of paper and a pencil and start writing it out. You're not submitting this to an art gallery, so beauty wins no awards here. Getting it out of your head and into a format that can be reviewed is the goal.

Questions to help:

1. What are all the places prospects find you? Referrals, searching Google, ads you run, tradeshows, outbound efforts, etc?
2. How do they reach out to you? Webform, phone, in person, social media, etc.?
3. How do they get a quote? Pricing table on your website, proposal, price sheet, phone quote, etc.?
4. How do they sign up? Order form online, printed order form, contract, etc.?
5. How do you provide them with what they paid for? Ship it, create it, meet with them regularly, etc.?

If you get ideas on how to improve what you see as you document your funnel, jot them down. Prioritizing them is key, so hold back and avoid the temptation to go down every rabbit hole you find. We'll go through how to prioritize and tackle the most valuable bottlenecks in Chapter 13.

Chapter 5

Traffic Pillars

"THE LOFTIER THE BUILDING, THE DEEPER
MUST THE FOUNDATION BE LAID."

— *Thomas Kempis*

If you've ever studied ancient history, you've seen the spectacular buildings from ancient Greece that are still standing today. The most iconic of the bunch is the Parthenon, which was finished in 438 BC to serve as the temple honoring the goddess Athena. Based on my math, that was 2,455 years ago, and it's still standing for all to admire. It even survived an explosion of ammunition that was stored inside it in 1687 CE.

The feature that stands out about ancient Greek architecture, and especially the Parthenon, is the use of pillars to create structures that withstand the ravages of time.

All the high-growth companies I've worked with share a similar feature with Greek architecture. Instead of physical pillars, they have Traffic Pillars that support the entire structure of the company. Without effective marketing, a business will only go so far, and will have a shaky structure.

The best example of this I've seen up close was with Business Breakthroughs International. I was the marketing director for the company started by Chet Holmes, who later brought in Tony Robbins as partner. Chet was a very talented marketer and initially built the company through his network and his ability to deliver great value to clients.

After he published his book *The Ultimate Sales Machine* in 2007, he began testing an advertising medium that most people wouldn't have considered, especially for a marketing and sales training company.

The medium was satellite radio, which consisted of XM and Sirius at the time. A friend in an agency was able to acquire remnant radio spots that were unsold by the channels. Like any perishable commodity, they are worthless if unused, so they are sold at a steep discount, making it a lower cost method to test if the medium is worthwhile.

Like most advertising, it wasn't a big hit at first. Chet was always a great copywriter, but the call to action (CTA) in the ads asked listeners to go to his website to get a free report. It didn't take long to figure out that most people listening to satellite radio are driving, so locating a website was difficult (as well as dangerous), and the listener usually forgot it by the time he got to his destination.

Chet tweaked the CTA so that it asked people to call an 800 number. The response was ten times greater.

As changes were made and the campaigns optimized, Chet was able to spend more money on them until we were up to more than $10,000 per week. We were generating interested leads at an average cost of eighteen dollars each, which included their name, phone number, and email for future follow-up.

When Tony Robbins joined, the first ads he recorded, reading the same exact copy Chet had always used, tripled our response rate. Our lead cost dropped to six dollars each overnight. His name recognition and instantly recognizable raspy voice were obvious assets.

Satellite radio became a Traffic Pillar for BBI and continued until shortly after Chet's untimely death from leukemia in mid-2012.

This experience showed me that one well-managed and optimized traffic source can build a company to at least $1 million in annual revenue, and even to $10 million and beyond like it did for BBI. This has proven true time and again with clients. The key is to find one Traffic Pillar that is the right fit for your business, matching your capabilities, resources, budget, and growth objectives.

Key Tip

I recommend staying focused on one Traffic Pillar until it generates at least $1 million in annual revenue before moving on to developing the next pillar. It is very easy to get distracted by the latest shiny new tool in marketing and have it stop your momentum.

Be persistent with your one Traffic Pillar even though it may eventually become boring. Just remember that it's the key to building a stable lead source for your business that will produce continued growth.

Think about the pillars of the Parthenon and how strong each one was as it supported the entire structure. Getting a Traffic Pillar to $1 million in annual revenue is equally as strong for your business foundation. Now think of how impenetrable your business will be if it has a half dozen (or more) Traffic Pillars, each generating at least $1 million a year in revenue.

Do You Have A Traffic Problem?

Many clients come to me thinking that they have a lead-generation problem. They are convinced that if they just had more prospects to work with, they would close more deals and make more money.

This is an easy trap for any stagnant business to fall into, just like raising capital can be for startups who think money is the perfect cure for their problems. They aren't sure what they would do with the money if they got it, or what issues it would actually solve. So, raising capital becomes the excuse for not doing the hard work of fixing problems elsewhere in the business. Lead-generation hacks and shortcuts have become the magical cure-alls, leading many business owners down the bumpiest of rabbit holes.

Even though getting more clients is a huge challenge for most companies, the vast majority of businesses have larger bottlenecks elsewhere that would become magnified with the addition of more prospects. That was the challenge for the marketing software company in Chapter 1 that didn't want to resolve their on-boarding and retention bottleneck.

Here are some quick questions to help you evaluate if you should be developing a new Traffic Pillar vs. optimizing what you already have in place.

ARE YOU AFRAID TO SAY "NO" TO BAD PROSPECTS?

If so, volume is likely low since you don't feel you can cherry pick the ideal clients. Go through optimization first to see if you can get more out of what you're already doing before implementing a new Traffic Pillar.

ARE YOUR LEAD COSTS CONSISTENTLY RISING?

This is typical of maturing channels like AdWords. Optimization is a must in this case. You should definitely start experimenting with new Traffic Pillars to provide more stability in the future if your current one becomes unsustainable from competition.

ARE THE LEADS COMING IN OF LOWER QUALITY?

This could be due to the fact that your lead source has lost high-value users and is now attracting the lagging adopters. Begin assessing if your message needs to be updated in order to stay relevant. If that doesn't solve the problem, then moving on to a new Traffic Pillar is wise.

ARE YOU GETTING REFUNDS, CANCELLATIONS, AND NO REFERRALS?

This is typically a sign that your fulfillment needs to be tightened up. In rare cases, your message may be flawed , attracting the wrong clients. If this isn't the case, then you'll want to fix your fulfillment issues.

A LIFETIME OF STUDY

If you feel a little overwhelmed with the barrage of options to advertise your business, you're not alone. Every single client that comes to me is in this exact state before we start working together.

The variety of ways in which you can generate leads for your business could fill ten lifetimes of study. There are thousands of blog posts, magazine articles, podcasts, books, workshops, and courses that come out each year covering the latest and greatest in the world of lead generation. And that's just the new stuff. Don't fear, there is hope!

The approaches that worked for the past 100-plus years are rarely discussed in this litany of new content, even though more than half of them are still completely relevant. You can make your head spin by adding the rapidly changing state of the Internet and how consumers are shopping and doing research online.

Needless to say, I don't have a silver bullet in this chapter that is going to help you multiply your lead flow exponentially overnight. Plus, you're probably tired of the empty promises behind silver bullets by now.

What I am going to do is build on the *Message-Market-Media* framework from the previous chapter to show you how to evaluate any lead source worth pursuing.

KNOW YOUR NUMBERS

John Wanamaker was one of the godfathers of modern advertising. He blazed the trail for the rest of us with his department stores in Philadelphia and New York back in the late 1800's. He invented the price tag and money-back guarantee, and he hired the world's first full-time copywriter, which he attributed to doubling his revenue from $4 million to $8 million.

Wanamaker is famous for stating the vexing dilemma all marketers struggle with: *"Half the money I spend on advertising is wasted; the trouble is I don't know which half."*

With the advances in tracking and reporting tools, the best marketers today are fixated on metrics, the numbers that tell you what's working and what isn't.

Wanamaker would be amazed by the tools we have today and would likely be an even more powerful marketing innovator if he were alive.

Before you consider any traffic channel, you've got to know some key numbers about your business. Without them, you're no different than an old lady dumping quarters into the slots at the casino, hoping to hit the jackpot. It is vital to know the following key numbers in order to make profitable decisions.

PROFIT PER SALE· We need to know how much you *net* after any given sale. This is not to be confused with what you charge per sale. You obviously have overhead, cost of goods sold, and other expenses that need to be covered before we start looking at marketing expense. If you're not sure what your profit is per sale, just start with the following formula:

NET PROFIT LAST YEAR (OR LAST 12 MONTHS) / TOTAL PROJECTS (OR UNITS SOLD) = PROFIT PER SALE

If you're not sure what your net profit is, you can simply use what's on your tax return, likely line 31 on the Schedule C.

CLOSE RATE· This is your batting average. This number tells you what percentage of new clients you convert from your lead pool. Most business owners overestimate this number by about double. If you think you're closing eight out of ten, it's probably more like four out of ten.

All you need to look at is how many proposals you made and then count how many of them closed. You can also look at how many people filled out a quote or inquiry form, and compare it to how many of them actually paid you.

Don't let your sales reps confuse the issue either by saying they close 100% of the leads that are actually qualified and capable of buying. That would be like saying they caught 100% of the fish that swallowed the hook. Lead quality is a factor in building a Traffic Pillar, but don't worry about this right now, as you'll optimize this later.

LENGTH OF SALES CYCLE· For most of my clients, the sales cycle takes more than one interaction with prospects before they become clients. They're not selling books on Amazon that people buy without a second thought. Sometimes I've seen them take as long as eighteen months, with others closing as quick as fifteen to twenty days. The key is to know your average sales cycle length, since that will determine how long it will take for your marketing budget to get paid back.

ACCOUNTS RECEIVABLE CYCLE· Getting paid is the most important factor in any business. Completing projects with delays in collections is a proven way to go bankrupt. This is called insolvency for a reason, since it has nothing to do with profits, and everything to do with cash flow. Right now, ask yourself how long it takes to get paid after your client receives your deliverable. Your goal should be less than thirty days. You should find a way to get paid before final delivery, typically with a sizable deposit when the project starts. There are no rules for these terms, just whatever you are willing to put up with.

CAPACITY: How many clients can you actually handle per month? So many business owners never think about this problem until they're flooded with more leads than they can handle. This sounds like a great problem to have, but it can actually backfire on you if you don't have a plan to handle the excess demand.

Also, once you reach capacity, how hard will it be to expand it? Do you need to hire more skilled staff to fulfill, or is it just a matter of adding a support rep for every 100 subscribers you add to your SaaS? Knowing these answers will help you determine how hard you can put the throttle down on marketing and what to do when the overflow of leads does come in.

CLIENT LIFETIME VALUE: Jay Abraham is the king of maximizing the profit from clients over your lifetime relationship with them. By focusing on this he has proven that you can spend more than your competitors in advertising to create the initial sale because you will make much more later on from their continuing business.

This theory is spot-on and has been used to build many empires. It is just a challenge for most business owners to calculate because they don't keep detailed enough records to pull from. Don't worry about knowing this number today. I'm just listing it here as an ideal to strive toward knowing and leveraging for all of your future marketing decisions.

Head to *bbg.li/metrics* to see example numbers with some comments on them as you pull together your own.

Traffic Fundamentals

Now that you know your numbers, you can move on to analyzing traffic sources. The nice thing is that there are only two categories that exist for generating leads: outbound or inbound.

Outbound is the umbrella term that covers any marketing effort that is sent out to capture the attention of prospects. This is predominantly traditional advertising that we all grew up with, such as radio and TV ads, door-to-door salesmen, direct mail, booths at tradeshows, pursuing RFPs, etc. It is synonymous with interruption marketing, capturing the attention of the prospect without them actively looking for it.

Inbound covers all marketing efforts that are done to make it easier to be found by those already looking or interested in a solution like yours. This is a growing form of marketing that has been expanded by the Internet and the growth of search engines like Google, making it easier for people to find solutions to their problems. It involves creating informative (and typically persuasive) content that prospects read, listen to, or watch as they investigate possible solutions for their problems.

This is most commonly created as blog posts, checklists, guides, recommendation lists, ebooks, webinars, demos, free trials, email courses, cheat sheets, etc. The list is long, but the goal is the same, which is to create something useful that builds trust and educates the prospect, moving them further down the sales funnel.

The difference between outbound and inbound is similar to the difference between hunting and fishing.

When an animal is being hunted, it is usually running away and hiding as much as possible. It's no different when a prospect is being pursued by advertising, especially when that prospect has shown no interest in what the advertiser has to offer. The key is to stop pestering them and approach them in a manner that they are receptive to. This reduces their fear and disarms them so they are not always on the defensive.

Fishing, on the other hand, is all about using a lure that is appealing and draws the fish toward it. You need to throw the lure *(message)* in an area where the fish are likely to be (*market* + *media* from the last chapter). It's still up to the fish (*customer*) to come to it. Like the juiciest worm for the fish, companies need to create great advertising and content to attract the prospect.

Just as hunting and fishing are both effective methods to put food on the table, there is no right or wrong marketing approach to building a Traffic Pillar that you rely on to make sales.

Yes, you can ignore the turf wars and hype between the inbound and outbound camps that fill forums, blog posts, and conferences defending their side. There are positives and negatives to both. It just comes down to the resources in your company and what is likely to work best in your market so you stand apart from your competition.

Also, don't fall into the simplistic view that outbound is more costly because you have to pay for the medium, or that inbound leads are free. Everything has a cost, whether directly by paying for clicks from Facebook ads, or indirectly, by taking your time to write a white paper to post online, hoping it will be found by ideal prospects.

At the end of the day, a good rule of thumb is to simply do the opposite of whatever your competitors are doing.

As Mark Twain said, *"whenever you find yourself on the side of the majority, it is time to pause and reflect."* This works equally well with what is going on in your industry and the marketing that dominates it.

Outbound

Like hunting for deer on the last day of the season by driving around in a pickup hoping to score a trophy, there are plenty of methods of doing outbound marketing that give it a bad rap. I find that the most egregious approaches to outbound never take into consideration how the prospect might want to be engaged. This creates an adversarial relationship that is only perpetuated by the automated cold calling that we all get, especially from *"Sharon, your local Google specialist."*

They interrupt your life and jump right into a full-blown pitch to try to hard close you in the first few minutes of meeting you.

I'm a major advocate of Seth Godin's method for doing outbound marketing, as described in his book *Permission Marketing*. Even though it was written in 1999, it is something I refer to frequently when working with clients.

In it Godin references the summer camp industry that ran ads in magazines for parents with pre-teen and teenage children. Everyone in that industry would cram as much text into a 2-inch by 2-inch ad, trying to make the case for sending your teen to their camp. It was a sea of sameness, and it was impossible for parents to make a decision about which camp was best for their kid.

Then there was Camp Arowhon, the oldest coed camp in North America, running strong since 1934. They took a different approach, moving away from selling their camp to parents in a 2-inch black-and-white ad. Instead, their only goal was to get permission to send parents a DVD and brochure for their camp.

Camp Arowhon's ad sells the info pack, not the camp. The goal of their video and brochure is to set up a meeting between the parents and a camp advisor to see if the camp is a good fit for the family. This stage sells the meeting, not the camp.

During the process, parents view testimonials, photos, the campgrounds, and happy campers. Camp Arowhon does this in person, because they know you're worth investing that extra effort. By following through with the face-to-face interview, they also get your permission at every stage of the application to keep going.

Camp Arowhon believes that there is a strong likelihood that your children will come back in future summers and bring a sibling or a friend. Godin estimates this type of enlightened outbound marketing was worth nearly $20,000 to the camp. All of this started with a simple 2-inch ad.

As you can see, at each step, the only goal is to expand permission to the next step.

By creating marketing focused on getting permission instead of making the sale, you will get a much stronger return on your marketing budget. Plus, your sales staff will be much more effective and happy that they're not chasing dead leads or being rejected 99 percent of the time.

You may be thinking that creating all these steps and related content is a lot of work right now. The reality is that your sales staff is already delivering this to every prospect that becomes a client, either verbally, by email, or in person.

Have your sales staff record their next sales pitch and get it transcribed (*bbg.li/transcribe*). This is the first step to helping your sales staff develop a polished new marketing campaign that is focused on closing more clients.

I expand further on this approach in the next chapter (#6 on Closing), so be sure to read that material carefully if this has captured your interest.

Inbound

A basic approach to inbound marketing is to create a simple report or guide that educates prospects on how to best solve a problem they have.

For example, offer "*5 Ways To Not Be Screwed By Your [Provider Type]*." Collect anonymous stories from clients on how other providers dropped the ball for them. Offer these stories to prospects as a download from your website in exchange for their contact information. This will help you build a relationship with them and eventually earn their business.

There are endless lists of options to expand on. Be aware that each type has a cult following that claims it is THE solution that you MUST do if you want to dominate your market.

Blogging was the top dog in the inbound marketing world for quite a while. My guess is that the age of bloggers peaked somewhere around 2012. Now we're fully into the age of podcasters, which will likely peak in 2017. Bloggers and podcasters have done their best to replace PR as the high-leverage trust-building channel of awareness to get in front of countless prospects. Fueled by Google's Search, iTunes' podcast distribution, and sharing on social media through Facebook, Twitter, and LinkedIn, these forms of inbound marketing have generated a lot of activity and a corresponding buzz in the business world.

Hubspot is a marketing software company that has positioned itself as the de facto pioneers of inbound marketing. They have built their entire system around helping companies create informative and persuasive content that helps attract, track, and close prospects.

They have made a convincing case for the effectiveness of inbound marketing, hosting a massive conference every year, at which they share information about the rapid innovation taking place in the inbound marketing world.

If you are like the majority of my clients, the thought of building an inbound marketing machine is completely overwhelming. And to be honest, I think it's unnecessary for 95 percent of markets out there. Unless you are in an industry where everyone has a big budget and a large marketing team, like enterprise software (Salesforce, Oracle, and SAP), you should be encouraged that just a little content can go a long way to generating quality prospects.

Combine Outbound and Inbound

The Permission Marketing approach I outlined in the example from Seth Godin about Camp Arowhon may seem like it has a lot of inbound marketing components in it, which come after the initial outbound advertisement. The DVD and brochure are informative, and the one-on-one consultation is requested by the parent, with zero pressure for closure.

Camp Arowhon's solution, combining outbound and inbound marketing, is the solution that I think works best for businesses of all sizes. By doing this, you gain the best of outbound marketing, which offers instant results and control over how many prospects you pursue and how many to close. Then pair it with the best form of inbound marketing, in which you educate the prospect, building trust and credibility in the process.

If you only use outbound marketing , you're going the way of Gordon Gecko*, as you try to play a pure numbers game to corral as many clients as possible.

If you go with a pure inbound strategy, you have to wait for awareness and results to start compounding in order to produce any measurable result. With inbound marketing only, you may start with the wrong content, audience target, distribution, or any number of factors, and end up wasting months (or years) going down the wrong track altogether.

By pairing outbound with inbound, you will receive quick feedback and thus will know whether you are heading in the right direction with the content, or if you need to make adjustments to better align with your target market.

---

* The classic hard closing, narcissistic character in the 1980's movie "Wall Street", played by Michael Douglas.

Creating Your Traffic Pillar

Before thinking about building a new Traffic Pillar, take into consideration that you might already have an adequate one in place. I recommend taking steps to optimize what you are already doing successfully before you try to replace it with something from scratch. The contents of Chapter 3 on optimization walk you through this process. The ROI is typically very fast and the risk of wasted capital is much lower.

When you start building a new Traffic Pillar, keep in mind that simplicity is the key. Don't get distracted trying to copy a mature marketing campaign from a competitor, as you run the risk of never launching it due to feeling overwhelmed. Getting it started is more important than trying to build something complex and perfect.

Here are questions I use to assess any Traffic Pillar, layering their answers over the *Message-Market-Media* framework to see which channels make the most sense to pursue:

CAN YOU CLEARLY DEFINE THE TRAITS OF YOUR IDEAL CLIENT? (MARKET)

Specificity matters here. Define every detail to create an ideal client profile, as if it were an actual person (or company) to direct all of your messaging toward. Create multiple ideal client profiles if you service different markets or project types, since you want to build Traffic Pillars for each market over time. Use the guide at *bbg.li/profile* to develop your ideal client profile(s).

CAN YOU CREATE A LIST OF SPECIFIC PEOPLE OR COMPANIES THAT HAVE A HIGH LIKELIHOOD OF MEETING YOUR CRITERIA? (MARKET)

I always prefer the surgical precision approach like a sniper, as opposed to casting a wide net and having to filter through lots of garbage and small fish that are a waste of effort. When I worked for Chet Holmes at Business Breakthroughs International, he called this approach his "Dream 100" since he found that targeting a list of 100 ideal prospects with laser-focused intensity always paid off. In my opinion, it's the most cost-effective approach, and it takes the least amount of effort, too, which is always a win in my book.

WHERE ELSE COULD YOU GET IN FRONT OF THEM? (MEDIA)

This is where Facebook and AdWords are so powerful, since so many prospects use them constantly. With the demographic data Facebook offers, and which AdWords is now including, targeting clients is much more efficient than the mass media channels of the past (radio, billboards, etc). There are also industry trade shows and publications, as well as influencers already embedded in that market, that can introduce you to a specific market.

HOW MANY LEADS MUST YOU GENERATE WITHIN SIX MONTHS TO REACH YOUR GOALS?

B2B businesses really shine here, because they can generate so much revenue from a single client that they don't need to attract thousands of leads to make a Traffic Pillar profitable.

HOW MANY MORE LEADS COULD YOU HANDLE IN THE NEXT YEAR?

What's your capacity to serve more clients once you get your Traffic Pillar in place? Do you need to hire more project managers, which are harder to source and on-board, or do you just need a customer service rep who only needs a friendly personality in order to be a good fit? This answer will help you see that you probably can't handle tenfold growth, so you don't need to build a Traffic Pillar that will generate 1,000 leads a day.

HOW MUCH MONEY DO YOU HAVE AVAILABLE TO INVEST IN THIS TRAFFIC PILLAR, WITHOUT NEEDING A RETURN ON IT FOR AT LEAST SIX MONTHS?

I'm a big believer in starting small and investing more as you are successful and see early indicators that show you're heading down the right path. Still, this approach requires capital, and you may not see any profit for a number of months given your sales cycle, seasonal fluctuations, and the fact that you may not hit the bullseye the first time. In fact, you should expect it to take three or four attempts to see some success.

Once you have answered these questions, you'll be equipped to review potential lead sources and begin building your Traffic Pillar.

There are a number of resources on the website (*bbg.li/book*) to help you evaluate possible lead sources, including worthwhile training on specific tactics that I know are effective and fairly priced.

ACTION STEPS

There may only be five Action Steps listed here, but each one will take time and effort brainstorming to help develop your Traffic Pillars.

1. Start by determining if you have a traffic problem right now. Go back to page 71 to answer the questions to find out.

2. Whether you do have a traffic problem or not, you MUST know your numbers. Go fill in your numbers for the metrics on pages 73 to 75. Save them for future reference. They are critical to know before starting any future marketing campaigns.

3. When you're ready build your next Traffic Pillar, start by answering the questions on pages 83 to 85. You will likely come up with many possible traffic channels.

4. Research what other companies like yours (or similar enough) have succeeded using each of the traffic channels. You are NOT looking to blaze a new, unproven trail right now.

5. Pick the first traffic channel to test and outline your implementation plan, including how you'll measure success. Start small. If you can build a brick, you can build a city, so it's ok to run a lot of cheap tests to see what works before committing more money to it.

This process can seem very tedious, but it's the source of tremendous scale and stability once you develop it. You'll keep coming back to this chapter many times over your entrepreneurial career.

CHAPTER 6

Closing

"IF PEOPLE LIKE YOU, THEY'LL LISTEN TO
YOU. BUT IF THEY TRUST YOU, THEY'LL DO
BUSINESS WITH YOU."

— *Zig Ziglar*

We've all known that guy who could talk his way out of any kind of trouble. Whether it was his charm, his disarming sense of humor, or the sincerity of his every apology, he rarely suffered the consequences of his actions. He could also convince you to do the craziest things. Whether it was climbing the fence and jumping off the high dive in the middle of the night or daring you to approach the prettiest girl at the party, he mesmerized you into action even though you were scared out of your mind.

Growing up, this was the personality I heard adults say would go far in sales, or worse . . . politics.

If you are like most of the business owners I work with, you don't quite fit this profile. You do just fine interacting with prospects and clients. Obviously, you have been able to get people to pay for your products or service, but you feel you could do better.

You may have even hired sales staff to try to find someone more capable to handle prospects. But as with so many companies, you've either faced chronic sales staff turnover or you're stuck with mediocre bench warmers. Even the headhunters who specialize in placing sales staff strike out more than half the time.

Like any other bottleneck, there are a few simple solutions that can unlock massive growth in your business through better closing.

I use the term "closing" because that is what the best salespeople focus on. The other activities traditionally associated with sales, including cold calling, canvassing, creating quotes, writing reports, forecasting, customer service calls, and territory management are all secondary to converting prospects into clients.

In fact, I recommend that you put into place more entry level staff, freelancers, and assistants to handle ancillary tasks, allowing you (or your sales staff) to focus on closing sales.

Sales Profiles

Before we cover the keys to improving your closing process, I'd like to discuss the worst sales profiles that just won't seem to go away.

We have all experienced the old school, fast-talking salesman. The guy going door-to-door selling solar systems on a Saturday afternoon. Or the guy with a booth at the fair selling non-stick pans. They have been around for hundreds of years selling snake oil, and we see them coming from a mile away.

Amazingly, that type of salesperson still fills used car lots, and they even work for major corporations like AT&T, usually in the "retention" department.

We'll call this profile Sleazy Sam. Nothing good comes of buying from Sleazy Sam. Buyer's remorse is the common outcome, giving you the same feeling after you agreed to help your friend move something, only to find out it was a dead body.

Obviously, since you're reading this, there's no way you'd ever sell like this, or allow anyone like this within a hundred miles of your company. Sleazy Sam doesn't read or work on improving his skills. His lack of self-awareness is the reason he keeps following this horrible approach to selling.

The next step up the sales ladder is the Objection Master. He has a canned response for every objection you offer. Some of them sound reasonable, and he always finishes them with a trial close because he still believes you should *Always Be Closing* (good ol' ABC). In the midst of his barrage, you provide a truly worthwhile objection, and he blurts out something ridiculous like, *"Do you have to check with your wife when you need to go to the bathroom?"* Instantly, you are snapped out of his hypnotizing routine.

He sees objections as if they're a pack of C-4 strapped to a cell phone awaiting a call from a crazed bomber. The faster he can defuse it, the safer he feels. The problem is that defusing objections is just fancy arm wrestling. You don't get anywhere and everyone feels exhausted by the end. Especially when he's always trial closing you.

This is definitely the method that gained fame in the 1980's, right along with the character Blake from *Glengarry Glen Ross,* and it still exists in far too many companies today.

The most common sales profile I see today is the friendly Golden Retriever, happy to chase down any ball you throw. They are the nicest people, loyal to a fault, and are easy to get to know. And as with a Golden Retriever, you feel at ease with them. Their biggest problem is that they are so eager to please that they help any and every prospect that comes across their desk. They'll waste hours answering questions from people who are just looking for info to take back to their current providers to negotiate a better deal, or from daydreamers who have no ability to afford your products or service.

Golden Retrievers also fail to demonstrate that your company is the best solution for the prospect. They never lead them to the fulfillment process, to show them that you will take care of every critical step. Prospects bail out on Golden Retrievers and their companies because they never feel completely safe. Somewhere in the back of their mind they realize that the sales rep doesn't know everything they need, and they aren't sure the company does either.

If you recognize some of these sales profiles in your company, or in yourself, you're not alone.

Sell Like a Surgeon

At the top of the sales mountain lives a once-rare creature that is, thankfully, becoming increasingly common in business today. He is warm and welcoming like a Golden Retriever, but he asks questions the prospect has never heard before. In fact, to get a meeting with him, the prospect has to jump through a few hoops first, to prove that they're qualified and worth his time.

The prospect schedules an appointment for an initial

discussion and the salesperson leads the conversation well, but he doesn't feel harsh like a drill sergeant. He outlines the next steps and schedules the next meeting before ending the first one.

This is the consultative sales pro, and if you pay close enough attention, his process is nearly identical to a surgeon's. He never pushes the product or service onto the prospect early, even saying things like, "*I'm not sure this will be a fit for you right now.*" He's comfortable saying "no" to prospects that he doesn't think would benefit from the product or service, just like a surgeon would say "no" to a patient who wouldn't benefit from the surgery they're asking him about.

The #1 goal in this role is to get on the same side of the negotiation table as the prospect to help them review their options, becoming a trusted advisor in the process. When you get into that role, if your product or service is truly their best option, they will sign up without hesitation because you've earned their trust at every step of the way.

You demonstrate your expertise by asking questions they've never been asked by any other company before. You haven't put your needs above theirs by pushing your product or service on them before finding out what their real needs are. And you've led them through a process they are confident you can deliver on, so they feel safe that they won't be left hanging after signing the agreement or paying you.

Many of the steps I just outlined may not come naturally to you, but that's OK because they weren't always natural for me either. Like anything new, you can learn to master them over time.

Head Game

Before deciding to go down the entrepreneurial path, I was set on being a surgeon. I sat in on knee and hip replacement surgeries with my orthopedist when I was still a senior in high school. When I worked in the ER for two years before applying to medical school, I helped all the doctors with as many procedures as possible. Whether it was straightening and casting a broken leg, holding a patient in the fetal position so they didn't move during a spinal tap, or assisting while they stitched up facial lacerations, I observed the doctors from the best seat in the house.

There were a few factors that separated the best physicians from the average ones that became very obvious over time.

The first was simply confidence. This wasn't arrogance, although a few definitely had that trait in spades. It was simply the ability to deliver a diagnosis and recommended treatment to a patient without floundering. Even if the patient was scared or second-guessed them, they would respond with a calm strength, reassuring the patient or answering their objection clearly.

Some of the doctors instinctively possessed this trait, but I also saw that they strengthened it over years and years of mastering their craft. The two most senior ER doctors I worked with were not only unflappable, but they also diagnosed conditions faster and more accurately than anyone else. This was mastery personified.

The atmosphere in the ER when these two doctors were working was always more enjoyable, too. Everyone followed their lead, and patients were treated and moved along as quickly as possible.

When a weaker ER doctor was in charge, everything changed. Patients became more restless and making a diagnosis took significantly longer because the doctors over-tested to be certain about a condition before prescribing a treatment. And the nursing staff was more chaotic, stepping in to take on additional responsibility in order to fill the gaps the doctors left.

The worst part of working with a weaker ER doctor was watching the stress bury them in the middle of a procedure. Most patients couldn't see this, given the position they were in, but I was front and center, watching them struggle to hold it together.

Like the best surgeons and ER doctors I got to work with, becoming a master at the consultative sales process starts in your head with your self-confidence. If you aren't there yet, please don't just "fake it until you make it." Nobody wins in that situation, and the stress you take on from it can be debilitating.

There are some great tips and techniques in the last section of the book on Mindset for beefing up your thoughts and emotions. Until you start seeing improvement in your mindset, use the following guide to help you make a huge improvement in your consultative sales skills immediately.

Consultative Sales Goals

Having read countless sales books, I've concluded that the vast majority of them just aren't worth reading. I list the select few that I recommend at *bbg.li/book* if you're looking for something meatier to sink your teeth into.

Compiling all the research I've read, as well as what works best for my clients, I recommend the following steps to successful consultative selling.

EDUCATE PROSPECTS WITH NEW IDEAS OR PERSPECTIVES

Returning to the subject of doctors as role models, this is one of the most powerful steps in their consultation with patients. They educate them about the need for the surgery, the benefits and risks involved, and what the recovery process will look like.

When I worked for a consultant named Chet Holmes [see Chapter 5], I was impressed by his commitment to education-based selling. He showed clients that companies that educate prospects increase their loyalty to purchase from them by 67%. That's a huge bump.

COLLABORATE WITH PROSPECTS

Becoming a trusted advisor is the natural result of collaborating with prospects. By asking questions to help them uncover the implications of their options, you help them see the situation from a more valuable perspective. The consultation moves beyond just dealing with symptoms and instead attempts to solve the root issue. When I've done this with prospects, it often uncovers other issues they didn't realize were contributing to the problem.

One client brought me in to advise them on how to improve their lead flow after launching their redesigned website. By considering a few questions about their redesign process with the website agency, we quickly realized the agency had neglected to go through some steps. It didn't take long to uncover the mess the agency had made and to show us the real issue why their website traffic and related leads had dropped off so much after the new site was launched.

PERSUADE PROSPECTS THEY WILL ACHIEVE RESULTS

This might surprise you, but the research is clear that buyers with large budgets count this as a positive trait of the sales people they purchased from. So many of us are conditioned to just say *"No"* when we feel the close coming on that we might dismiss it as necessary. This isn't so much about pitching the prospect on the benefits of a solution, but rather giving them a level of certainty that moving forward will lead to a positive outcome.

Certainty is a fickle thing to dole out. It has an inverse relationship to experience, since the more experience we get, the more we know the many ways things don't work out. The ignorant are typically the ones making proclamations with the most certainty. It is called the *Dunning-Kruger Effect* and can be seen in the chart below.

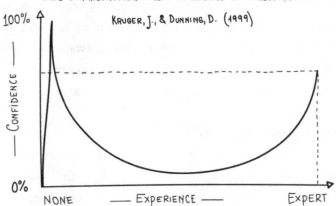

DUNNING-KRUGER EFFECT

UNSKILLED AND UNAWARE OF IT : HOW DIFFICULTIES IN RECOGNIZING
ONE'S OWN INCOMPETENCE LEAD TO INFLATED SELF-ASSESSMENTS

KRUGER, J., & DUNNING, D. (1999)

The solution for you is that once you cross the chasm from ignorance to mastery, you have historical data to rely on, just like any good surgeon. That's when your track record becomes the anchor for persuading clients of the positive outcome they can anticipate. Until then, I find that stating the possible pitfalls, and how they'll be handled if they come up, provides enough certainty for most prospects to pull the trigger.

LISTEN TO PROSPECTS

We all know that listening is one of the most valuable traits in building strong, healthy relationships. Unfortunately, this is my greatest weakness in the consultative sales approach, and I know it bleeds over into other parts of my life. Thankfully, I'm effective enough with the other components to make up for this one, but I'm finding that it is just as important to master the skill of listening as the other four skills.

If you're like me, you have a hard time listening to everything someone is saying because your mind is racing ahead to the solution. Or it could be that you get bored easily. Whatever the reason, I've found that repeating what the person is saying in my mind keeps me focused and present in the conversation.

It takes some work at first, but it is the best way to short-circuit my racing thoughts and boredom. Plus, it has a very calming effect, and I find I start enjoying the conversation much more.

UNDERSTAND THEIR NEEDS

This skill takes a bit of empathy and strategy to really master, because you need to be able to put yourself in the prospect's shoes, while also seeing their bigger picture. There's nothing more infuriating to me than hearing about clients who bought a solution because the sales rep said whatever they thought it would take to make the sale, regardless of the fact that it wasn't useful for the client.

I understand the need to make quotas, meet shareholder demands, and feed your kids, but relying on *caveat emptor* (buyer beware) as the mantra for your sales approach is abusive at best and criminal when you get into the land of Madoff and Belfort.

I'm against regulation, but at times I really wish there were repercussions for abusive vendors like there are for surgeons that push unnecessary procedures on patients. The tech and marketing spaces can still feel like the Wild West, and ignorance abounds on the client side, making them vulnerable to rip-offs.

Put these five components together in your sales efforts, and prepare to enjoy the increased close rate that results. It really is the easiest and most fulfilling method of closing new clients.

Proposals That Win

If you've been in business for more than a few years, you probably have a sufficient stream of inbound prospects that keep you afloat. The ones that develop into customers are like solid base hits; they keep the game moving along steadily and productively, if not with dramatic results.

Every once in a while you get an inquiry from a massive prospect, like a hospital in the midst of building a new wing, or Google looking for a team they can outsource some development to. You drop everything to try to land them, but either feel overwhelmed because there are so many details to their proposal or indifferent because you think your chances of landing this super-prospect are slim-to-none.

From the one out of ten deals like this that you end up landing, you get a glimpse of where things could go in your business if you could just close them better. It's definitely a Catch-22, since you know there are more deals like this out there, but you can't afford to keep spending time on them when you only close one out of ten.

I've found that the single greatest method to improve your close rate on larger projects is to deliver a proposal that cuts through the clutter and differentiates you instantly in the application process. That's how you massively increase your close rate.

10x Close Rate

As I discussed in chapter 4, Yamabe & Horn Engineering had been in business for over 30 years, successfully providing civil engineering services to local municipalities and developers. Some of the projects they worked on transformed rural towns, from providing safe, clean water to creating innovative community parks that were the first of their kind in California. They even helped their municipal clients secure federal grant funding for the projects since their city budgets were too strapped for anything beyond the bare necessities.

Having survived the recession with minimal damage, by 2012 Yamabe & Horn wanted to pursue more projects to kick-start their firm's growth. They began submitting proposals to cities that had published Requests for Proposals (RFPs) and Requests for Qualifications (RFQs) on projects they needed done.

One of the senior engineers took on the task of reviewing the RFPs and RFQs and then creating the proposals (or statements of information for RFQs) for them. Over an eighteen-month period they pursued 54 RFPs and RFQs, but only secured four of them in the process (a success rate of 7.4%).

Then, in late 2012, their largest municipal client decided to put their feet to the fire due to the need for more innovative and adaptable project management. They opened up a competitive RFP process to the market. Yamabe & Horn realized they needed to pull out all the stops to keep this client since it accounted for a significant percentage of their annual revenue.

A major pillar in landing the contract was to deliver a stellar proposal that would impress every person in the decision process by answering every question and highlighting the benefits that Y&H brought to the table as their civil engineering firm for twenty-one years. This was a concern to Y&H since many of the decision makers were new to the city staff.

The challenge in creating robust proposals was that Y&H had very little content to pull from regarding their capabilities and skills. It had to be drafted from interviews with the principals and key project managers. To compound the challenge, the deadline for delivery of the completed proposal was only three weeks away.

Over the following three weeks we were able to create a comprehensive thirty-two-page proposal that not only highlighted the firm's talent and the investment in technology they had made, but was also presented in the form of an impressive full-color, saddle-stitched book.

The decision makers at the city were impressed with the entire approach and awarded Y&H the contract for the next three years, amounting to a seven-figure contract.

To generate further benefit from the effort, we took the comprehensive proposal and repurposed it into various templates to use for other RFP/RFQ submissions. The result was a proven template that has led to success in over 70 percent of the projects they have pursued since. It has not only saved the Y&H staff time and effort, but has resulted in a steady flow of new projects and new relationships that they can leverage going forward.

If you would like help creating a proposal template that wins, go to *bbg.li/proposals*

ACTION STEPS

Just like everything else we've covered, to improve your sales process you need to start by first defining what you're currently doing.

1. Write out the steps you take prospects through to become clients. If you have a star salesperson that closes more than everyone else, have him write out his steps, too.

Once you have your process outlined, answer these questions to help assess whether you're achieving the consultative sales objectives:

1. Are you taking too long to earn the prospect's trust?
2. Are you just quoting prices, instead of determining the prospect's needs?
3. Are you failing to ask questions that demonstrate your expertise compared to your competitors?
4. Are you failing to persuade prospects that you can deliver their solution with confidence?

Based on your answers above, finish by:

1. Going through the five steps of consultative closing on pages 94 to 96 to see where you can add those pieces into your process.
2. Writing out the new and improved steps to your sales process.
3. Sharing with your sales team and training on it weekly (using the outline on page 136).

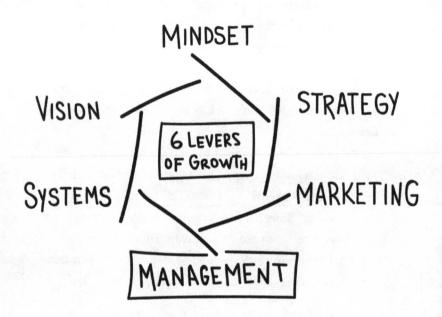

Management

> "GOOD MANAGEMENT CONSISTS IN SHOWING
> AVERAGE PEOPLE HOW TO DO THE WORK OF
> SUPERIOR PEOPLE."
> —*John D. Rockefeller*

Management is consistently undervalued in small businesses, while it can be overvalued in Fortune 500 companies. Based on the scorecard of profits, the Fortune 500 win this argument.

Small business owners equate the topic of management with bureaucracy, creating unnecessary oversight and slowing down implementation in the process. The problem with dismissing the topic is that it becomes a significant bottleneck preventing growth at many revenue plateaus.

The simplest definition of management I have found is:

*Directing and equipping people to accomplish goals
by using available resources effectively.*

Viewing management through this simplified lens helps strip away the negative bias toward it and makes it much easier for most owners to tackle.

Since small business owners resist working on their management skills, I have developed a few key management hacks that generate quick, sustainable results. They reduce the owner's frustration, while also unlocking the potential in their staff or, if necessary, helping them replace underperforming staff with better players.

The beauty of improving your management skills with the strategies shared in this section is that your company will grow more smoothly, allowing you to hire full-time managers for the different departments sooner. This releases you from day-to-day management responsibilities as quickly as possible.

It really is counterintuitive for most small business owners, since they are repulsed by the structure and rigor of management, but the quicker they master it, the quicker they are freed from it.

If you end up hating the process of improving your management skills, just remember this great quote from Winston Churchill: *"If you're going through hell, keep going!"*

Chapter 7

Management Basics

"The productivity of work is not the
responsibility of the worker, but of
the manager."

— *Peter Drucker*

In 2006 I had a mortgage brokerage that I was trying to grow
into more than just a two-person business. We had the process down for getting loans approved with relative ease, and I
closed prospects well, so I did what so many do at that stage
and started hiring more staff. I had failed at this a couple years
earlier when I was fresh out of grad school and jumped into
the mortgage business during its heyday in 2004.

This time would be different because I was so much more
experienced. Plus, I had a steady stream of clients coming in
from numerous referral sources. I hired a dedicated loan processor, a graphic designer to help with marketing, and even landed
a few interns from the local university (to do what, I wasn't sure).

The excitement was high for a few months, but then the
reality set in that there was a lot of activity but no real growth.

There was just more cash going out the door than before. I didn't have a clue that each staff member needed clear job responsibilities, so I would give them vague instructions and hope that everyone would figure out what to do.

To be honest, I didn't know how to set priorities or stick with a plan long enough to get it off the ground. I was a total visionary who could see 10,000 steps ahead, but didn't know what to do next to turn it into reality.

Needless to say, by August 2007 when IndyMac Bank went under, the wheels were already about to fall off. I think the credit crisis saved me from a long, slow death and mercifully put me out of my misery by early 2008.

Since then, I've realized that I made every mistake in the book, and I've seen most business owners make them, too.

If you're like most of my clients, the topic of management is pretty low on your interest list, somewhere between taxes and root canals. It is mundane to me, too. Unfortunately, mastering management is required to build a successful company.

This chapter explains the hacks I have created over time to make management as simple and effective as possible so it would stop being a bottleneck to growth for my clients. You could say that they are the bare minimum I could come up with to solve management bottlenecks so I could keep working with clients on strategy and marketing opportunities. Like most hacks, they work surprisingly well and can take you much further than you would expect.

I guarantee that you will never see most of these hacks published in a management journal or taught in a professional development course. But if management has become the bottleneck that is preventing your company from growing, I know they will help you.

In the next chapter I'll go over the single activity that will let you implement all of these hacks in one step, making it as easy as possible to get results. But don't skip ahead until you read this chapter and identify at least one mistake you're making right now. The activity I'll describe in Chapter 8 will work better with a clear bottleneck to fix.

Unstated Expectations

In early 2007, two of my employees managed to see the writing on the wall and abandoned ship on the same day that I happened to be leaving for a long weekend at a conference. My wife offered to jump in and help, thinking she could alleviate some of the stress I was buried under at that point.

It was our third year of marriage and, looking back on it a decade later, was clearly the toughest one by far. If I expected employees to just figure out how to do their job, my expectations for her were ten times higher. I had a short fuse because my ego was so wrapped up in being an entrepreneur. When she would come to me with concerns that the ship was taking on water, I exploded. I had a freakin' MBA in entrepreneurship, so there was no way I was going to admit defeat.

As the pressure of working together was about to crush us, we sought counsel on how to make our marriage healthier. When I was trying to figure out why we were fighting so much, a conversation with a mentor led me to the label of "Unstated Expectations."

It was the perfect term for what we kept running into in our marriage. I expected her to do whatever I demanded at work, and she expected me to listen to and respect her. Obviously, the issue was on my end, but without stating these expectations, we were setting each other up to fail.

That phrase transformed our marriage.

Since then, it has been our go-to solution when we start getting short with each other. We check in and see what unstated expectation the other has, and it diffuses the situation instantly. We both know we can't be mad about the other person not being able to read our mind.

I believe that unstated expectations are the cause of most friction in all relationships, whether marriage, parenting, friendship, or work. When we expect something of another person that they are not aware of, and they don't meet it, all manner of disappointment sets in.

I see this with my clients all the time.

Business owners have the habit of believing that how they think is "common sense," and that it is handed out to everyone like candy on Halloween. They think it's "common sense" to show up on time, to call ahead if you're going to be late, to double check all of your grammar in email communication, and never to yell at anybody on the phone. Their list of unstated expectations is seemingly endless.

Regardless of how skilled, experienced, smart, or attractive an employee is, if you're not stating clearly what you expect from them on a daily basis, any failure on their part to perform is 100 percent your fault. I know you might have a million examples where their failure to use "common sense" created a bad outcome in your company, but it's your job to lead and manage, and that involves giving clear instruction.

A good rule of thumb if you're expecting staff to read your mind or use "common sense" is to count how many times you get frustrated with them in the course of a week for not getting something done. If it happens more than zero times a week, I guarantee you're not being clear enough on what you expect them to do. Without telling them the rules of the game, there's no way you can judge them for not scoring.

If you feel like this situation is turning you into their parent, keep reading.

Change Your Perspective

An employee I fired after only a few weeks of working with us filed for unemployment and listed my company as a past employer. The EDD sent me a notice of the claim, so I responded with my case that she was warned multiple times for her bad attitude. I even mentioned that she admitted she should be fired after the final confrontation. They still ruled against me because I didn't produce three reprimands signed by her showing that she was given a fair chance at resolving her character defects to try to keep her new job.

Needless to say, I was furious. I told a mentor that it felt like the EDD viewed every employer as though they were as ruthless as Steve Jobs, and every employee as though they were a helpless third grader (I used a few more adjectives for emphasis). She wisely told me to let it go and move on, but the Jobs vs. third grader analogy stuck in the back of my mind.

I started wondering what would happen if I viewed employees like third graders (or 8-year- olds). It's a funny exercise, but it unlocked something pretty amazing for me.

First, as I write this, my oldest child is 8, and I would never expect her to know everything that I know, but she is capable enough to be given directions and to follow them. Her brain is developed enough to connect some obvious dots, but I wouldn't expect her to pull off the high-level strategic deduction that I do every day to solve problems (although she definitely surprises me with some of her insightful observations).

At my mortgage brokerage, I started viewing my employees as 8-year-olds, and after only a couple weeks I had an epiphany. I was no longer frustrated with them.

Honestly. All of my previous frustration with them vanished.

I was more willing to explain how to do things. I coached them more, instead of snapping at them when I saw something that could be improved. I had more patience with them, and they seemed to appreciate all the changes in me, too.

Whenever I tell clients to try viewing their employees like eight-year-olds, it always gets a chuckle because they think it's a joke of some kind. I'm also waiting for the day when an employee catches wind of it and he punches me in the face for suggesting it.

Really, there's no disrespect in the perspective shift for me, as I don't think I'm better than they are or that they're stupid. It just helps me see that they need more support at times to do their job better because I know significantly more about running every part of the company than they do.

If somebody with 20 years' experience shows up, and they

are finishing your sentences because they're so knowledgeable, then you might try viewing them at the stage of a 12-year-old. They have more experience and may know how to do X, Y, or Z, but you still want to validate it. Double check their deliverables while they earn the trust to have more responsibility and autonomy.

NEVER trust any new employee based on face value, even if they have great referrals. This isn't because you should be a cynic. It's just a proven recipe for disaster three or six months down the road, once you realize they were failing miserably because you weren't double-checking them occasionally.

Regardless of how experienced they might be, they probably don't do things the way you do. Trust me on this one, and give it a shot.

Top Function of Management

If we view the role of management as being sandwiched between the front-line employees they're directing and the owner they're reporting to, then there is only one key function management fills: equipping staff to do their job.

> There is only one key function management fills: EQUIPPING STAFF TO DO THEIR JOB.

As I've said earlier, small business owners rail against the topic of management because they think of it as the bureaucracy that permeates big business and government.

Paring it down to the idea of helping staff do their job causes it to become immediately valuable to them. It also makes it easier to keep managers more accountable for their performance.

While managing staff, a common bottleneck shows up when staff aren't completing their tasks. Realizing that there are only two reasons someone doesn't do their job helps clear the bottleneck, and avoids all of the excuses in the process.

1. They don't know how to.
2. They don't want to.

When they don't know how, it's the manager's responsibility to provide the training or the tools they need to do it. My recommendation is that every time you teach someone how to do something that might be done again by anyone in the future, write it down and save it in a Google Doc. I even use screen capture software (*bbg.li/screenshot*) to record the steps and save it with the document. This becomes the foundation for systems that we'll cover in the next section.

When someone doesn't want to do a task, it could be due to an attitude problem or their personality not being a good fit for the task. If they excel at certain tasks, but perform poorly at others, then it's likely a personality issue, and it would make sense to find someone else to do the tasks they hate. In the case of an attitude problem, I find that explaining how the task is valuable to the company on a larger scale can help them see the significance of their role and to develop some team spirit. Most employees want to contribute to what matters in the company, so give them a chance to see how their tasks do that.

If the employee is just a prima donna and doesn't want to do the job, then you need to decide if they're worth making an exception for or if they need to be given an ultimatum.

Personally, I have a lot of grace for top performers who can be high maintenance at times. They're almost like savants, delivering massive results in the things they're great at, but worthless outside of their area of genius.

Priorities

Most employees have more on their plate than they can handle. The recession led many companies to discover that they can get by with less staff, requiring the remaining employees to be more productive. The problem I see repeatedly is that the owner doesn't communicate priorities enough with their staff.

This leads to employees completing tasks based on two criteria:

1. Whatever is easiest
2. Whoever they're most afraid of disappointing

There are a lot of tasks that are easy to do, but don't move the needle at all for the company. Whether it's filing paperwork, calling maintenance to fix a leaky faucet, ordering office supplies, or any other mindless task, it's easy to fill many hours with them.

Then there are tasks that employees complete out of fear. Typically, they're afraid of one of the co-founders in the company more than the others, or they want to stay on the good side of a key employee, doing their bidding even if that employee has no authority to direct them.

The solution to both of these issues is to help employees prioritize their tasks. Telling them what you expect instantly cuts through their uncertainty. Plus, I find that the majority of employees love to get this kind of clarity from you. It lets them focus 100 percent on completing the right tasks so they stop wasting their mental energy on second-guessing whether they're doing the right thing. Decision making is exhausting, especially when you don't have the authority to go with it.

Responsibility + Authority

As a business owner, you've probably never noticed the balanced relationship between responsibility and authority. That's because you have complete control over both. You own the business, which makes you 100 percent responsible for its survival, and you have 100 percent authority to make any decisions that would increase its chances for success.

The people who do notice the relationship of responsibility and authority are those who don't possess them in equal amounts.

Every case I have ever seen of a responsibility and authority imbalance happens when an employee is given the responsibility of creating a specific outcome, but doesn't have the authority to do what is necessary to make it happen. This isn't quite Hell, but it sure is close, so I refer to it as Employee Purgatory. It's like Sisyphus being responsible for rolling the rock up the hill, but not having the authority to build a platform to store it once he gets there, so it keeps rolling back down.

Imagine a marketing director who is responsible for capturing leads on the website for the sales team, but who doesn't have the authority to fire the incompetent web development team. Every time the marketing director makes a recommendation to the website team they botch it and end up breaking other parts of the website. The marketing director is blamed for the website issues his requests cause and for not generating enough leads, even though he is not able to do anything about it because he lacks authority.

This type of situation is the fastest path to employee burnout because the stress of responsibility without the authority to ensure competent performance is unbearable. I believe this one imbalance is a major contributor to more heart attacks on Monday morning than any other day in the week. I would not be surprised to learn that it contributes to two of the top three causes of death for people aged 35 to 44, suicide and heart disease.

To uncover where you are giving employees responsibility without authority, just pay attention when they come to you for approval to implement solutions that will help them do their job. Start giving them more authority to solve problems on their own, extending it over time as they prove capable of handling it.

My favorite way to do this is to ask them, *"What do you think you need to do this right?"* When they answer with something you approve, say, *"Great! Go for it. And you have authority to do this without my input in the future."*

You'll instantly notice that the *"got a minute?"* meetings drop significantly, and employee attitude will dramatically improve with the added trust you've given them. It really is a win-win. Plus, the chances of them getting a heart attack next Monday will go down, too.

Org Charts

For most of my clients, the idea of having an organizational chart seems like the start of a slippery slope to bureaucracy. As the owner, you fill every role out of the gate anyway, so creating a chart just to put your name on it is a pointless exercise. At some point (typically $500k/year), it makes sense to start organizing all the tasks, and group them into some logical categories to develop staffing positions around.

As you might guess, these categories then become the foundation for roles in an org chart. It's just the logical outcome from making sense out of the chaos that comes from running a business.

Every company outside the Fortune 500 struggles to keep employee roles and responsibilities clear. This is especially true in companies under $1 million in annual revenue, since everyone on the team is likely capable of performing a variety of tasks, able to roll up their sleeves and jump in to get stuff done anytime.

Things start breaking down when there is no clear assignment of responsibility for a task, resulting in things falling through the cracks because someone assumed someone else was going to take care of it. As the owner, it's your responsibility to clarify roles and assign tasks and responsibilities.

A lot of organizational management philosophies have appeared over the past couple decades. As famous and charismatic entrepreneurs become billionaires, publishers flood the market with books about them that claim they will show you how to duplicate their success. I'm not going to cover any of those approaches here because I don't think outlier celebrity cases are duplicable.

With that said, let's dive into the process of getting some role organization in your company in order to make it run better.

The fundamental design of org charts shows that every employee has one clearly defined boss.* This is shown by the line going from their role to the one above it. This may seem obvious in companies with fewer than ten staff members since everyone deals directly with the owner. Once you get beyond this stage, clarity about supervision can pose serious headaches if you are not aware of, or operating by, it.

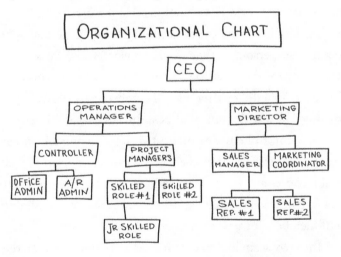

Let me tell you about a CPA I know. He is one of four partners in the firm, and they have around twenty staff. It was early April, and he had to go out of town for a meeting with a big client, but still had a mountain of tax files to prep and review before the 15th. Before he left, he delegated

---

* A person in charge of a worker. It could be "supervisor" or "manager", but I think boss defines it best.

two important tasks to two different people, giving them clear instructions and deadlines for work that needed to be completed before he returned.

When he came back to work, he found that neither of the tasks had been completed. Both staff members made excuses about other things having come up and not being able to get to the work. Needless to say, the partner was livid about this and had to work incredibly late for two nights to complete the work before the deadline.

I asked him what he did to confront their failure to deliver, and he said he couldn't do anything. He felt handcuffed.

The problem was that staff members were not accountable to a specific person. So they would do whatever was easiest or whatever kept the most frightening person away. In this case, the senior founding partner was the only one who always got his way. He was the unstated boss, but he was semi-retired at this point, so he wasn't interested in managing anyone or directing their work. The other three partners were left to pick staff favorites and hope they would deliver, but they felt completely paralyzed when it came to confronting or disciplining staff members if they failed to perform.

This may seem like an extreme example, but I see it all the time in companies with more than one owner.

The solution is to give every employee a boss, typically one of the partners, and have that boss handle prioritization, support, and discipline, regardless of who delegated the task. It can be tedious having to go through your partner to confront an employee who left you hanging, but the increased accountability and clear path for discipline is worth it in the end.

The other benefit of giving every employee a boss is that when an employee gets overwhelmed with tasks from different superiors, it gives them a place to go for help prioritizing it all. As I said earlier, deciding on priorities is a major source of stress. Helping alleviate that stress results in employees delivering more quickly and with higher quality every time. And this works especially well in cases where employees receive tasks from multiple sources.

A key point about the one-boss-per-employee approach is to make sure that you are not undermining the structure by bypassing someone's boss and changing the priorities or disciplining front-line staff directly. This is a recipe for confusion and eventual conflict between you and their boss for not following the agreed-upon structure. In the end, you'll have increased freedom to run the company when you follow it, so just let go of the need to control everything, and it will work for you.

Another argument against org charts is that you don't have enough employees to fill every role. The reality is that most employees wear multiple hats. So just put their name in as many roles as they are responsible for. You'll find that your best staff are doing a number of things, in some cases spreading themselves too thin but still managing to deliver fairly consistently.

This can be a huge lever to pull. It will get your top staff more focused on the key activities that actually move the needle and will eliminate lower priority tasks. One client found that a top-performing engineer on the team was stepping up to manage relationships with key municipal clients exceptionally well. But he was also doing a lot of basic design work that could be handed to CAD designers. They ended up making him the lead engineer for their largest client, which allowed him to apply his relationship and strategic planning skills, tripling the revenue from that client in the process.

Identifying his greatest skills and reassigning all the low-priority tasks was worth well over a million dollars in new revenue to the company.

Stinky Fish

As a consultant, I find myself trying to boil down advice as much as possible to simple, easy-to-understand concepts so my clients will remember them and take action. This leads me to use quips and catchphrases that I end up repeating endlessly. A side effect is that my wife gives me grief for how many times she's had to hear them over the years.

One phrase that I find my clients repeating back to me more than any other (and warming my heart every time) is:

"The fish stinks from the head down."

This is the word picture I give them any time they are complaining about a dysfunction in their company that is a result of their behavior as the leader. I sell it to them as an old Chinese proverb to help it stick a little better, even though every nationality throughout history claims to have originated this aphorism.

In essence, you create everything in your company as the leader of it. Good or bad, it's all your doing.

A great example I always mention is the client who had invested over $40,000 into a CRM (before they worked with me, of course, since I would have steered them to something more practical). Two of the owners of the company were the top people in the sales department, which had five additional sales staff. While I was helping them with their marketing plan, I asked for a report from the CRM to see how they were tracking lead sources to better analyze what was working and what was a waste of time.

To my surprise, they gave me a batch of spreadsheets that had been maintained by an assistant, completely outside the CRM, and with no lead source tracking. Scratching my head, I asked why they couldn't pull the reports from the CRM directly, and was told that the data in it was unreliable since it wasn't used very much.

Neither of the owners used it, and there wasn't a sales manager in place to force the sale staff to use it either, so it just sat there, completely ignored. One partner didn't like the accountability of having to input everything, so the employees followed his lead and gladly avoided the accountability, too.

You can imagine the implications of not using the CRM, from horrible forecasting for use by their production team in their planning to no lead scoring or analysis of their long sales cycle (the spreadsheets contained limited data because they were manually maintained by the assistant). Plus, the cost of an assistant to maintain the spreadsheets was around $20,000 a year.

The greatest irony was that the partner who pushed to get this CRM deployed was always complaining that they needed a better system, and was constantly chasing the latest shiny new object in the market, wasting time with demos and proposals.

A common and worthwhile leadership approach is to never ask your employees to do something you wouldn't be willing to do yourself. This is a good rule of thumb, but it falls apart quickly when you get into specialized activities, especially rote and detailed tasks that most entrepreneurs aren't wired for. Regardless of the dysfunction you're trying to resolve, the key is to identify your behavior that is enabling the dysfunction and to short-circuit that behavior.

In the case of the client with the $40,000 CRM, one of the partners hates documenting things and refuses to update his prospects and pipeline using it, so he should just have his assistant do it so they can include his numbers in their forecasts and reporting. Then they need to require the sales staff to keep their leads updated to the same standard, or better. Having accurate data will improve their analysis and allow them to make better decisions, putting the investment in the system to good use.

ACTION STEPS

In the next chapter I'll go over the single activity that will let you implement all of these hacks in one step, making it as easy as possible to get results.

Before you dive in there, answer these questions:

1. Where do you have *commonsense-itis* (coming in Chapter 11) that causes you frustration with your staff?
2. When was the last time you trained someone how to do a key part of their job?
3. Who have you given responsibility to, but not authority to do what's necessary to get results?
4. What bad behaviors are you modeling that allow your staff to skate-by because they're just copying you?

CHAPTER 8

Weekly Implementation Meeting

"MANAGEMENT BY OBJECTIVE WORKS ...
IF YOU KNOW THE OBJECTIVES. 90% OF THE
TIME YOU DON'T."

— *Peter Drucker*

In 2003 a couple of HR executives at Best Buy started experimenting with ways to improve productivity and employee satisfaction. In the process they created some very effective innovations in the management world, resulting in the model they named the *Results Only Work Environment* (ROWE).

Plainly defined, it said that employees could work whenever and wherever they wanted as long as they delivered results that were agreed upon between the manager and the employee.

So what happened when Best Buy implemented ROWE? Employee productivity in this Fortune 500 company increased by 35 percent. Even more impressive was that voluntary employee turnover went down by 97 percent. Clearly, the employees loved this new model, and the company profited from it, too.

Like anything that bucks the norm, there was a lot of resistance to this approach from leadership in other companies when they assessed whether to implement it. Comically, the most common gripe about ROWE was how to account for vacation and sick time benefits since those became obsolete once anyone could work, or not work, anytime they wanted.

The biggest challenge I have seen for any company implementing ROWE is that it requires management to clearly define what employees are actually responsible for and measured on. For the most productive employees, the slippery slope was having more work piled on to fill the proverbial 40 hours a week they owed the company. To combat this, ROWE forced companies to define very clear scope and performance metrics for everyone.

This model is very challenging to implement, especially in growing companies where the tasks and priorities are in a state of constant evolution. If you think about it, most business owners end up relying on employees as a kind of indentured servant. *"Show up for 40 hours a week and do whatever I tell you to do"* is the common edict.

I'm a big advocate of ROWE, but I would never suggest trying to tackle it until your management fundamentals are securely in place. The reason I have highlighted it here is to help set an ideal for you to strive toward as you try to improve your management skills. How great would it be if you could get to a point where your employees were as productive as they could possibly be, while loving their work so much that they never thought of looking for another job?

As I said in the last chapter, I've found a single activity that helps solve all of your management problems, while also setting you up well to move toward the ROWE model in the future if you want.

Weekly Implementation Meeting

As the title suggests, the activity is a weekly implementation meeting one-on-one with each of your employees. Now don't start whining that you don't have the time to add these meetings to your already full schedule. I guarantee you'll get back at least three hours for every one you invest in these meetings.

And if you're not looking forward to meeting with certain employees because they're abrasive or you just don't get along, then I'd suggest diving into Chapter 9 on confrontation after this. You're the owner and it's up to you to create the ideal environment you want. Remember, the fish stinks from the head down.

Before we dig into the structure of these meetings, know that the benefits are numerous. I've seen employee productivity go up dramatically, fires reduced so you're not walking around like a reactive firefighter all the time, and owners empowered to effectively discipline staff. Moreover, you will gain time that you can use to focus on strategic initiatives or simply claw back to have a life outside of work.

First Meeting

As with almost anything new, the first one is always the most difficult. If you've had a culture with no accountability to this point, there will likely be a few blowups by staff as they start feeling uncertain about their place in the company. Even the most mild-mannered employees can lose it, just like Pinky the cat did in this adoption video (*bbg.li/pinkythecat*). So be prepared for some blowback as you start down this path of accountability.

Going back to eliminating unstated expectations, this is a great time to over-communicate why you're implementing this change and what your goals are for it.

All you need to say is something as simple as this:

"Hey team, we're at a point where I know my management skills need to improve to help us grow. So I'm following some advice that I know has worked with other companies like ours, and I'm going to start having one-on-one meetings with each of you every week. It's going to be a great time for both of us to talk about what you're doing, what you need from me so you're as equipped as possible, and any ideas you have that could help improve the company. And don't worry, this isn't some elaborate setup to start laying anyone off or replace you. I just know that I need to improve my management skills, and this is the easiest way to do it."

I recommend batching all of the meetings so they are back-to-back on the same day every week. They typically don't last more than 30 minutes, so if you have six direct reports, you can knock them out in less than three hours. That's only 5-10 percent of your entire work week, and it's one of the most productive activities you can do, so make the time and stick to it.

In your first meeting with each employee, you won't have anything from the prior week to review, so you can just jump right into establishing a baseline for their role with the company.

If their role is not clearly defined, then that's the best place to start.

I like starting with statements like the following:

"Let's put everything on the table that you've been doing over the past few months, and start organizing it into a clearer list of responsibilities. To be honest, we might find that there are some things you've been doing that should be given to someone else. In the end, I want you to be doing what you do best."

Then, get out a piece of paper and start jotting down tasks that both of you can think of. Don't spend a lot of time trying to include every activity, since they can be added later. The weekly implementation meeting is a system, so it is more like a marathon than a sprint. It will evolve.

From that list of tasks, you will likely see some patterns that will provide a basis for organizing them. The employee might have been paying bills, calling clients with outstanding balances, answering the phone, ordering office supplies, and answering customer questions that come in through email. From this list of tasks, they appear to fill three different roles, which include bookkeeping, office management, and customer service.

I've had situations like this where the employee was clearly capable and interested in one role more than the others, even though she was hired for another role. We shifted her to the new role, where she thrived, while passing the other tasks over to others who enjoyed them more.

Once their role is clearly defined and agreed upon, you can then find out what they need to do it better. I simply ask:

"What do you need from me to make your job easier to do? You have full immunity to say whatever you want, and I promise to keep it between us if it involves someone else in the company. You can bring up anything you think would make the company better, too. And don't worry about forgetting something important here, because you'll be able to bring this stuff up every week in these meetings."

Get ready to listen and write a lot of information down. Most employees have a lot to talk about because they have bottled it up over the years.

I keep a spreadsheet on Google Drive that lists any idea that can't be implemented immediately. I also include the name of the employee who came up with the idea so they can get credit if it turns out to be a winner.

The final topic for the first meeting is to talk about what their priorities are for the next week. If they have not kept a list of to-dos up to this point, then you'll want to write some out with them in the meeting. I'd suggest reviewing their email inbox, too, since it's probably full of things waiting to be done. Otherwise, have them grab their to-do list and bring it to the meeting. Go through it with them and mark the most important tasks you want them to complete before your next meeting in a week.

An important step that might not seem obvious is to let them know why these top tasks are so important to the company. Every employee wants to be of value, so if you can tie any task you give to them to some greater outcome that it helps support, you're going a long way to increasing their personal feelings of value.

One disclaimer I give everyone when starting this process is:

"To be transparent, I'm not sure how hard each of these top tasks are, so if they end up being too much to handle, don't worry that I'm going to be upset next week when we review them. Really, I just want to figure out how much you're capable of accomplishing over time so we are both better at predicting what's realistic in a week. I don't want to end up just burning you out by burying you all the time."

I find that this takes a lot of pressure off employees who are eager to please, but not vocal enough to push back when they need to, especially since I have a very dominant personality.

Be sure to write the top three to five tasks you prioritized for them in the weekly implementation meeting template so you can have them at your fingertips in the next meeting. Download it here: *bbg.li/meeting*

At this point, you just need to ask them if they have any questions before wrapping up the meeting.

These first meetings might take longer than thirty minutes each, but it's worth every second you invest in them to set the stage for the new weekly implementation meeting system. The better you kick off this system, the more momentum it will carry, increasing your chances of successfully continuing it.

Ongoing Meetings

Once you get going, the agenda outlined in the template above will drive everything.

I recommend printing a new template every week for each employee and keeping it in a folder that is used for these meetings. We'll revisit this folder later in the chapter, but you'll need a new weekly implementation meeting sheet to start every meeting with.

The first thing to check on is the status of the top priorities from the prior week. This is not the time to focus on discipline or disappointment if they weren't done. I'm not suggesting you just let them off scot-free, but the last thing you want to do is hammer them for not performing while you're trying to get this weekly implementation meeting system up and running.

Be sure to write down the status in the first box on the sheet, so you can see what's not getting done from week to week. This will uncover patterns down the road that are only visible by writing these uncompleted tasks down.

Then, ask the employee what prevented them from completing the task(s).

This information will most likely lead to other areas you'll need to fix in their role, particularly if they're being inundated with distractions or fires they have to put out. It may also shine a light on their lack of ability or knowledge about how to actually perform the tasks, which will provide you with the opportunity to train them. Or as occasionally happens, they will end up admitting that they hate the tasks and aren't wired for them like they thought they were. In which case, you can decide whether to reassign those tasks to someone better suited to completing them.

Whatever the reason, these are all positive data points to uncover so you can work to resolve them and set the employee up for future success.

If they got all their tasks done, then I'd suggest stepping up the game a bit by assigning them more challenging tasks. The following statement is a useful reminder at this stage:

"Remember, I don't want to just keep piling stuff on you, but I do want to find the happy medium where you're feeling challenged and delivering on important things for the company. So what do you think about adding XYZ this week?"

If they are unsure, don't pressure them. You can ease into it after they have a few more successful weeks and feel more confident in their abilities.

The goal here is positive reinforcement, so it's all about encouragement and providing a vision for seeing more of the potential that you see in them.

After you review their task completion, move on to asking them what kind of support they need from you. This may already be clear from the previous section if they couldn't get their tasks done, so don't feel that you have to force something here.

However they respond, be sure to write it in the box on the implementation meeting sheet since it will reveal patterns over time that will help you see blind spots where you're not providing your employees what they need to do their job well.

Then work with them to set their priorities for the next week. Remember to write these down in the box so you have something to refer to in the next meeting. They should include whatever tasks rolled over from the previous week that are already at the top of this sheet. Feel free to change priorities anytime. You're the boss, and what matters today is what's most important at all times. Don't let what is written down on this sheet dictate your priorities.

Between Meetings

David Allen is a thought leader in the productivity field, having written the timeless bestseller on the topic, *Getting Things Done*. After reading his book in 2005 in an effort to learn how to stop being a full-time firefighter at my mortgage brokerage, I went to one of his two-day workshops.

He told a story about a business owner who had paid his princely $10,000 fee to spend two days with him to learn how to get his life back in order. David followed him around for the first day, making recommendations where possible, and watching the owner's life be sucked dry by one *"got a minute?"* meeting after another.

To start the second day, David made a recommendation to create folders for each of the 15 employees who reported directly to the owner. They set up a file rack (like this one: *bbg.li/filerack*) on his desk and filled it with the folders. Then he grabbed a stack of loose sheet paper and put it right next to the rack.

He told the owner to write down anything he wanted to review with each employee on those sheets and stash them in the related folder. Only one topic or task per sheet. Then, five minutes before each one-on-one meeting, he would pull the employee's folder out and go through his notes from that week to prioritize them and review with the employee as part of the meeting.

David said that the owner went from working sixty hours a week, feeling out of control and in reactive mode, to only working two days a week, batching the fifteen meetings across both days. Everyone was more productive and the owner could tackle more strategic initiatives with all of his newfound free time.

I was clearly sold on the concept and have used it with employees and freelancers ever since.

I ended up using scrap paper, cutting it into quarter sheets that were 5.5" by 4.25" and stacked up nicely next to my phone and pen holder for quick access. Obviously, the paper type and size doesn't matter, as you just need to capture the thought.

The best part of the weekly implementation meetings is that you can force your employees to save their *"got a minute?"* requests to be handled in those meetings. It's amazing how many interruptions you can eliminate when you have a place for those requests to be handled.

You'll have to train your staff on what is actually a fire that needs your immediate attention. It's a great opportunity to show them that it should have gone on their list of things to review with you during the next weekly implementation meeting. Or it could be an opportunity to tell them that they have the authority to deal with the problem without your input.

You may notice that the weekly implementation meeting template includes a fourth box at the bottom that wasn't addressed in my meeting outline above. That's where you include the items captured throughout the week in their folder.

Discipline

To be honest, I dislike disciplining employees. I may come across as a bit gruff or blunt, but my empathy is too high to lay into someone when they don't deliver. One of the better surprise benefits from the weekly implementation meeting system is the fact that you can actually discipline employees in a clear, healthy manner. Since they're agreeing to complete the tasks you're helping them prioritize, accountability is very clear. Managing by agreements removes any uncertainty around your expectations, and their only way to avoid being accountable comes down to their excuses, whether reasonable or fabricated.

I've also found that nearly all employees beat themselves up more for not coming through when they agreed that they would. This is usually all the punishment they need to shape up, and it frees me to be an encourager who helps them focus on coming through next time.

If you've ever been in the situation where you felt powerless and hung out to dry when an employee fails to deliver, then the weekly implementation meetings will solve that for you in short order. Plus, the meetings help build your HR documentation should you need to fire the employee.

Additional Benefits

In addition to all of the benefits listed above, there are a few more that are great to keep in the back of your mind so you exploit them as much as possible.

The first is the ability to keep your finger on the pulse of your company. There's nothing more frustrating than to uncover a major issue or cancer in your company after it has wreaked havoc for months and months. One client of mine found that her bookkeeper had been stuffing bills in a drawer without opening them. It wasn't until suppliers started emailing the owner asking for payment months later that she uncovered the issue. The worst part was that the company was very profitable and could pay the bills on time with ease. It was simply laziness by the bookkeeper, who was subsequently fired, leaving a mess to clean up that could have been caught with a weekly meeting.

Another benefit is the ability to track progress more accurately. We entrepreneurs are an optimistic bunch, so we tend to put a rose-colored filter on everything. Exaggeration is common, as is feeling like things are growing faster than they really are. By having these weekly implementation meetings, you will better calibrate your optimism closer to reality, which will help you make better decisions.

Custom Meetings

If you have others managing key areas of your business, I suggest adding some specific details to your weekly implementation meetings with them. It will make your time with them that much more effective, and is also likely to eliminate the need for other meetings you have with them.

BOOKKEEPER

I think this is the most important meeting, but it's one that business owners neglect all too often. Whether you feel intimidated by accounting reports (specifically the Profit & Loss Statement), or it just bores you to review this stuff, you need to put on your big-boy pants and get over it. This is a critical area you need to keep in check, especially while your business is growing. It's very easy for cash flow to get pinched with big invoices outstanding, while you continue to pay bills and payroll, draining your bank account in no time.

The Profit & Loss Statement should be on a cash basis, not accrual, so you can see what was actually received as income for the month, as well as what was spent. Cash is the lifeblood of your business. You're not filing your taxes on this report, just monitoring the health of your company.

I recommend reviewing it by the 10th of every month for the previous month. So, in your implementation meetings, make sure it is part of the recurring priorities for your bookkeeper.

You should also review Accounts Receivable every week to see what invoices you are waiting to be paid on so they don't fall through the cracks. You're not a finance company. Make it a priority to keep everything well under thirty days and call clients at least twice a week for payment once they start running up against that timeline.

SALES REPS / MANAGER

If you have sales staff, reviewing their pipeline is the top priority during your weekly implementation meetings. Write down their forecast estimates on the implementation sheet and review them regularly to see how accurate they are. You'll notice trends and can help them improve the accuracy of their forecasts over time, which will give you great insight into upcoming growth.

In addition to getting the sales reps' status updates on each lead, I like to do some roleplaying with them to keep improving their engagement and closing skills. It doesn't have to be every week, but if you find them stalling out with certain leads, share how you would approach them or brainstorm an approach together, and then have them practice going through it with you acting as the prospect.

Finally, if their pipeline is light, brainstorm some lead sources for them to pursue. Maybe they should check in with current or past clients and see what testimonials or referrals they can get from them in the process.

MARKETING

Depending on your marketing staff's skill and responsibility, the following advice will need to be adjusted to match it.

Marketing directors today function more like project managers over the various vendors, freelancers, and software needed to implement a comprehensive campaign. If you have them committed to building out your Traffic Pillar, then everything should be focused on the next steps of implementation and how they are tracking that implementation.

You should be getting data on how much they spent, how many leads were generated, how many of those turned into qualified prospects for sales, and how many were closed.

Helping them see the upcoming steps in any campaign so they can effectively manage them is a huge benefit you can provide in these meetings, too.

If the employee is only responsible for a piece of marketing, like managing the email list or creating proposals, then you'll want to include data from those areas as part of the meeting with them. This could be open rates, click-through rates, inquiries, and unsubscribe requests for emails across campaigns, or it could be in-process, delivered, closed, and stalled for proposals.

ACTION STEPS

Follow these steps to start your weekly implementation meetings today (or tomorrow at the latest).

1. **Get the template:** Add the weekly implementation meeting template to your Google Drive or download it to save on your network here *bbg.li/meeting*.

2. **Talk with staff:** Tell them what you're doing and why. Use the script on page 126 earlier in the chapter if you need some guidance.

3. **Schedule meetings:** Get them on the calendar and batch them back-to-back. Even if you can only fit in fifteen minutes for each one tomorrow, get started.

4. **Print template:** Print a copy for each employee and use it for your meeting with them.

5. **Create meeting folders:** Create a folder for each employee to store the weekly meeting notes in, as well as topics to cover that come to mind during the week.

If the crazy roommate in your head is coming up with all sorts of excuses why you can't get to this right away, tell it to shut up, and push through to get it scheduled. The more you want to resist this, the more you need these meetings.

CHAPTER 9

Confrontation

"YOUR SUCCESS IN LIFE CAN USUALLY BE
MEASURED BY THE NUMBER OF UNCOMFORTABLE
CONVERSATIONS YOU ARE WILLING TO HAVE."

— *Tim Ferriss*

Your largest client just submitted another project to you, and said they need it delivered in half the time you think it should take, but they promised it shouldn't be nearly as complex as the last one. To top it off, they're sixty days late paying the final half of the last project. They are very responsive to all your emails and calls about current projects, but they ignore any email you send about their outstanding invoices or respond to it weeks later when they finally decide to cut the check.

It feels like you're locked in a prison, but you're too scared to try to escape. That is, until you explode and "go postal" on everyone within earshot. Or worse, you simply stop showing up and let everything fall apart around you, while you self-medicate with some not-permanently-damaging vice.

If you're anything like me, you've grown up with a healthy dose of altruism burned into your subconscious. We're taught that putting others' needs before our own is a worthy character trait, and I don't disagree with that. I just think it gets severely distorted, especially when used as a method of control or manipulation.

When you pair altruism with empathy, which allows us to put ourselves in their shoes, you've got a recipe for chronically taking the short-end-of-the-stick in all areas of your life, especially your business.

The cherry on top of the altruism + empathy combo occurs when you act as a peacekeeper, too. You do whatever you can to keep everyone happy. The problem is that you end up sacrificing your happiness <u>every single time you do this</u>.

The answer is not to become a raging asshole, trying to channel your inner Jordan Belfort to get your way every time.

Instead, I suggest that you learn to get comfortable with confrontation.

Every great leader and entrepreneur I've ever studied accepts that confrontation is to be expected. And every person I've ever seen who fails to step up to their fullest potential hides from it. It's that simple.

Purpose of Confrontation

I was doing some work for a friend's business a few years back and had a meeting with his partner at the end of the project to tie up some loose ends. In the course of the meeting, I discovered that my friend had lied to me about when they would be paying my final invoice. It was one of those things that leaves you dumbfounded, questioning what on earth the motive could have been for it.

After stewing about it for a couple days, I knew I needed to confront him to clear the air. During the time I was mulling it over, I stumbled onto a gift. It was the realization that the only purpose of confrontation is to resolve dysfunction. You have to do whatever is possible to restore health to a relationship.

> The only purpose of confrontation is to resolve dysfunction. You have to do whatever is possible to restore health to a relationship.

In addition to removing the dysfunction, confrontation also frees you from the endless mental loops that eat away at your focus and energy as you try to deal with it. Once you bring it into the open, it gets diffused almost instantly, regardless of how the other person responds. You may have new challenges if they decide to attack you in return, but the turmoil they put you through while stewing over it loses its power.

The fascinating thing in many cases of taking the short-end-of-the-stick is that the person inflicting their dysfunction on you doesn't give you a second thought. While you brood about all the ways you've been wronged, disrespected, and generally taken advantage of, they're moving right along without a care in the world.

Bottling up your negative feelings to keep the peace really does become a prison. It's completely self-sustained, because the key to unlock the cell door is in your hand at all times. You just need to muster up the courage to confront the person you let imprison you.

Courage

When building my own confrontation muscle, I found myself coming up with many excuses to avoid it. I'd think, "I'll confront them if they do this again," even though it was already the umpteenth time. Or I'd tell myself, "I don't want to confront them since they are already burdened by so much." I'm sure you have many excuses that sound reasonable, too.

In the end, it just comes down to taking action even though we are afraid. That's what courage is.

Mike Tyson's famed coach and father figure, Cus d'Amato, has what is, in my opinion, the best perspective on handling fear.

"What is the difference between a hero and a coward? No difference. Only what you do. They both feel the same. They both fear dying and getting hurt. The man who is a coward refuses to face up to what he's got to face. The hero is more disciplined and he fights those feelings off and he does what he has to do. But they both feel the same, the hero and the coward. People who watch you judge you on what you do, not how you feel."

I still feel the butterflies in my stomach before confronting someone. They are definitely not as strong as they used to be, and I'm no longer short of breath and flush in the face, but they haven't gone away completely.

After studying top business leaders for the past decade, I now know they all feel these things, too. They just decide to act in spite of them because they know that inaction accomplishes nothing.

Hacking Courage

There are a handful of ways I've found to muster up the courage to confront someone or do anything that makes me fearful. They all come back to shifting my perspective away from the immediate, to step back and take a more long-term view of the situation.

The first is simply to ask the question, "What's the worst that could happen?" In most cases, this is all I need to ask because I know that the odds of completely destroying the relationship are essentially zero. When it comes to confronting clients, my fear is always that they will decide to stop working with me. In 100 percent of the cases in which I've confronted clients, that has never happened. The relationship has always improved.

Over time, you will find the track record of confrontation starts building enough trustworthy data points that you can start recalling those to kickstart your courage before you even have to ask yourself the question.

The next step in hacking courage is a little more complex. It comes from my belief that life is always working things out for my ultimate benefit. You may completely disagree with me on this.

I've just found from my own personal experience that even the most painful, catastrophic, and bad things still weave together to create something better later on. Whether it's been bankruptcy, foreclosure, a miscarriage, being in the ICU from a head injury, or blowing the MCAT (which prevented me from getting into med school), I can see now how they all led to positive outcomes later.

If you've never looked back at the catastrophes in your life to see how they either unlocked something better later on, or were the crucible to strengthen something in you that has made your life better now, I'd encourage you to take a stroll down Memory Lane. I'm confident you will see that everything ended up working out in the end.

With that perspective, I can step back and see that resolving the dysfunction in my life right now will always produce more fruit later on. If it means that the relationship with the person I'm confronting comes to an end, I trust that it's opening up space for a new relationship that is better for the new season I'm stepping into.

Early on in my confrontation muscle-building pursuit, there were times where those two hacks still weren't enough for me to take action. I found that the question, "Why is their joy more important than my joy?" was the key that would finally get me unlocked. This question has a lot of layers, so here's why it worked so well for me.

First, it short-circuited the excuse to not add more of a burden on them. It helped me see that I was taking the short-end-of-the-stick again. Plus, I knew that if I was stewing over it, taking away my joy, that my wife and kids were getting emotional shrapnel from it, too. It's impossible for me to stay my positive, fun-loving self with my family when I'm mulling over the frustration of something I need to confront.

Sometimes I can talk it out with my wife and defuse it without having to confront the person, but that's just a Band-Aid™ until they do it to me again. In the end, asking "Why is their joy more important than my joy?" shows me that not having courage hurts my family. This allows me to overcome any reluctance I have about acting through my fear.

How To Confront

Before you charge off to confront every person causing turmoil in your life, here are some tips that will help you avoid stepping on landmines in the process.

First, do not take their actions personally that triggered the dysfunctional relationship. I know that's a million times easier said than done, but the reality is that very few people intentionally want to cause you grief. They are acting out of their own stress, and it just happens to point at you.

IN PERSON

Avoid confrontation through email or text. There is no end to the ways in which the written word can be misunderstood, and the last thing you want is a misunderstanding over something this important. I have used email to set up a confrontation call so the other person isn't completely sideswiped by it when I bring it up in our next conversation. But I never fully explain it or try to resolve it through email.

Here's an example to give you some context.

I was helping a client launch a completely new offer to their email list. It took a few months of research, testing, and building everything out before we were ready to launch it. Then, during the launch, he disappeared on me twice, not responding to email or Skype messages for a full week the first time and five days the second.

I was completely hand-tied waiting on him both times. Obviously, my frustration was sky high, especially since he had put the deadlines together with me and I wasn't going to be able to meet them now.

Instead of blasting him through email, I sent him the following message:

"Hey,
Not sure what's on your plate right now, but I need some input on the next promo email before I can move forward. If you could spend 5 minutes going through it and leave any comments on it, that will allow me to get it out the door.
Then we can discuss updated timing on our next call so we're on the same page."

Let me break this down so you can see my thinking behind it:

I start by acknowledging that I'm sure he's tackling some big stuff that's causing him to check out. Most people have no idea how their actions affect others, so I just want to help him see that I understand, but still need a response.

Then I give him very clear instructions that will help me get unlocked. This sets up the confrontation to show him that I didn't need hours and hours of his time to keep moving this forward. It helps defuse his potential argument that he didn't have any time available for me, because he can find five minutes anywhere.

Finally, I let him know that we're going to be updating our agreement regarding what's expected because his delays set me back two weeks. This is the very mild tip-off that I will be confronting him on this, without making him get all worked up or defensive.

POSITIVE THOUGHTS

The worst results I've ever experienced during confrontation came when I was still angry, to the extent where I even wanted revenge while I was doing the confronting. This just buries any positives that come from the confrontation with so much negativity that the only outcome is more conflict. It's like you take the negative feelings you're carrying and pass them over to the other person to be multiplied in the process.

I'm sure this is how civil wars have started.

The only way confrontation works to produce a healthier relationship is if I come at it without any anger or desire for revenge. I have to be 100 percent focused on resolving the dysfunction to make the relationship healthier. I'll even explain this to the person I'm confronting if I feel they're starting to get defensive. It gives them instant perspective and takes away nearly all the tension instantly.

Since I need to be in a peaceful, positive state when confronting someone, it usually means I need to sleep on it. Very rarely am I able to identify the exact issue that's causing me stress right in the moment and then deal with it on the spot. I think that's a superpower worth developing, but I am not quite there yet.

When you are triggered through email by someone else, that makes it 10 times easier to want to confront them through email. Don't Do This. It's the worst kind of trap, and will just lead to a downward spiral if you do.

FAST TALKERS

I've come across situations where the person who needs to be confronted is a master at avoiding it. A brilliant counselor friend of mine talks about how some people develop the ability to keep any bricks thrown at them from ever reaching the target. The mental bricklayer takes anything coming at them that might cause them any harm or discomfort and diverts it off to the side to build a wall of protection.

The master bricklayers in our lives always seem to have an excuse, objection, or way of deflecting our statements so that they are never held accountable for their actions. They can even make us feel bad for trying to confront them, too, which is always a tip-off to know they've mastered the art of deflection. Another tip-off is if they seem to be faster at processing the conversation than I am, using false logic to trip me up and escaping before we can resolve the confrontation.

It's like dealing with a master litigator who is always pummeling me in court, much like Johnny Cochran did to Marcia Clark in the O.J. Simpson trial.

The way I've found to confront the fast-talking bricklayer is to start by confronting the dodging tactics themselves or being much more blunt out of the gate. The following are go-to statements that have worked for me. Your mileage may vary.

"I'm not enjoying working with you, and I want to change that."
"I don't care what your excuses are. We are going to talk this through until it's resolved."
"I know this isn't fun for you, but if we're going to continue, it needs to be resolved."

The other pitfall when confronting a person like this is that they start trying to throw bricks back at you. When that happens, I've found the following response works to keep the conversation on point:

> *"We're not here to talk about that right now. I'm happy to go over it with you later in this process, but right now we need to talk about XYZ."*

Who Do You Need To Confront?

As a business owner, your list of possible confrontation sources is longer than most. You interact with more people than the average person, and you carry more responsibility, too. Since this book focuses on helping you grow your business, the following are the key roles and possible triggers that justify a confrontation.

EMPLOYEES

A business coach I worked with once coined the term "thick air" when I was dealing with a difficult employee. She said that if anyone working for me created tension anywhere in the company, then they had to be confronted to resolve it. She called that tension thick air, and it defines the situation perfectly for me.

You feel it the second you're in the same room with them. You avoid eye-contact, or talking about trigger topics, or even adjusting the conversation you're having with someone else when they're around. Regardless, you know the feeling of thick air, and you need to confront it.

The beauty of confronting employees is that it can happen effortlessly in your weekly implementation meetings with them.

CLIENT

Dan Kennedy told me a great line that will help you know if you need to confront a difficult client. *"If I wake up in the morning thinking about you more than two days in a row and you're not my wife, then you've got to go!"*

How many times do you go to bed or wake up anxious about a difficult client? No amount of money is worth that stress. Plus, as I stated above, every time I've confronted clients that were causing me this anxiety, it was resolved without any backlash or damage to the relationship.

A great way to start the confrontation is to let them know that you've been stressed about the relationship. I start with a disclaimer like, *"I'm sure you have no idea this is happening, but I've been worried about X for a while. I just need to get it out in the open and figure out how to resolve this so it's no longer a problem on my end."*

The majority of the time, they'll respond with surprise, and if they're really healthy, they will apologize and encourage you to bring up this type of problem sooner if it happens again.

If you're dealing with stressed-out employees of a massive client, then you might not get very far with this approach. They're likely to throw their hands in the air and reveal that you're only feeling a fraction of the stress they've got from managing unrealistic expectations from their boss or department.

In those cases, I find that what works best is maintaining strong boundaries and over-communicating what you need from them in order to perform your job. I have a client who works with a massive client and who ended up dealing with delay after delay on the client end, but they wouldn't allow him to change the delivery date in the contract. He obviously felt the stress since the delays just meant more pressure for his staff to deliver on time, which was unfair to everyone involved since the contract had been negotiated months in advance.

The solution was to send contract amendments documenting that the client was failing to hold up their end of the timeline. This would allow him to justify a later delivery if his team needed the extra time. It also triggered a new clause in future agreements that kept the delivery date flexible if the client didn't deliver on their responsibilities.

PARTNER

Business partners can be harder than marriage partners at times. You are tied to them until death (or buyout) do you part, but you don't have the love and lifelong commitment as a foundation to work through difficulties. And you don't have time alone at night after the kids go to bed to talk through things so you can get back on the same page.

The issues above involving "thick air" and waking up thinking about these problem people usually go hand-in-hand with partner conflicts. In every case I've advised, the partner with the anxiety is the one taking the short-end-of-the-stick, while the other partners aren't aware of it, or are master bricklayers themselves.

Whatever the case, you owe it to yourself to resolve this issue as soon as possible. Letting business-as-usual distract the two of you from dealing with this is as bad as ignoring that brain tumor that's giving you headaches every day. The conflict will grow rapidly and eventually kill you and/or the business.

If your partner isn't responsive to your confrontation attempts and is happy to protect the wall they've built, then you need to enlist professional help. If you can't find a consultant or business mentor to facilitate the resolution, then going to a marriage and family counselor or talented life coach would be next on my recommendation list. You need to do whatever it takes to get this resolved. Otherwise, you're just subjecting yourself to living with a thorn in your side until you or your partner get a business divorce.

VENDOR

The easiest way to know if you need to confront a vendor is if they are not making your life easier on every front. If they deliver late, screw up orders, have batches that break or are low quality, or have terms that cause you stress, then you need to confront them.

The goal of every vendor relationship is to be mutually beneficial, but that's not always the case. If you're a small fry in their pool of clients, then obviously you can't go in guns blazing, demanding that every concession be on their end. But you can certainly let them know that specific parts of your relationship aren't acceptable and see what options they might be open to for improvement.

As Wayne Gretzky famously said, *"You miss 100 percent of the shots you never take."* I tell every client in this situation, *"You don't get what you don't ask for."*

Don't forget that this may be a good time to review whether new vendors now exist that weren't around when you started working with the one that's giving you a headache now. I know that change can be tedious, but removing the stress is always worth it, and you never know what new benefits might exist with other vendors that could open new doors for you.

Obviously, your life extends far beyond the boundaries of your company, so don't stop with this list to improve your relationships. It can be emotionally exhausting to clean up dysfunctional relationships, so just chip away at them as you can. It's not a race, and I think you'll find plenty of motivation once you see how great it feels to clear up some of the more toxic relationships in your business.

ACTION STEPS

Who is causing you stress in your life right now?

That's the first person you need to confront.

Take some time to write out the factors causing you stress. Also, be sure to include the solutions to these problems so that you can present them.

Then muster up the courage to confront them.

I always recommend just walking into their office at the end of the week when things are slowing down. Or take them out to grab a cup of coffee. If it's an employee, do it during your Weekly Implementation Meeting with them.

Scheduling the confrontation ahead of time and making a big deal out of it tends to magnify it unnecessarily. You're not going to trial, you're just resolving a relationship issue.

Once you get one confrontation done, I'd suggest continuing to do it until all of your relationships are back to good health and are no longer causing you stress. If the problem is with an extended family member, it might not be possible to resolve it, so use your best judgment to decide whether it's worth confronting them.

But issues with everyone in your business and immediate family must be resolved now that you have the tools to do so. Life is too short to put up with dysfunctional relationships and the stress they cause.

Systems

> "NINETY-FOUR PERCENT OF PROBLEMS IN
> BUSINESS ARE SYSTEMS DRIVEN, AND ONLY
> SIX PERCENT ARE PEOPLE DRIVEN."
>
> — *W. Edwards Deming*

If marketing grows a company, then systems sustain it. They are the perfect one-two combo to continued growth.

Systems allow momentum to build, eliminating the waste of reinventing the wheel every day. They also allow you to upgrade staff as efficiently as possible, reducing the downtime while you take them through the on-boarding process.

This bottleneck starts becoming chronic at the $1 million plateau, and it becomes toxic if not dealt with by the $5 million mark. Getting past every growth plateau requires continual attention to developing systems, just as marketing does.

For most owners, the idea of developing and documenting systems is as exciting as a colonoscopy. This is ignored by most systems-focused training since much of it is created by people who love systems.

Like the management section we just covered, the next two chapters are focused on the simple hacks I've used with clients to get them to benefit from documented systems and the resulting ease of delegating tasks because of it.

Chapter 10

Systemize It

"Systems permit ordinary people to achieve
extraordinary results predictably."
— *Michael Gerber*

As I've mentioned earlier in this book, nearly every one of my clients came to me with a marketing need, typically focused on generating more leads to help grow their company. In roughly half the cases, they actually had a systems problem or, better stated, they didn't have anything documented to keep from having to reinvent the wheel every day. It also interfered with their ability to easily assess the performance of their activities, since their systems documentation was locked up inside everyone's head, and clear metrics for each staff member were non-existent.

A pattern developed where I saw companies grow through marketing and then need to consolidate that growth by documenting and optimizing the systems created from it. This process goes right along with the pattern of growing revenues first, and then optimizing them to maximize profits from that growth. It's incredibly difficult to try to accomplish both at the same time.

Like other disciplines in the business world, systemization has developed quite a cult following over the past 30 years, starting with Michael Gerber's *The E-Myth*. In it, Gerber makes the case to develop such robust documentation and systems that your business could become a franchise prototype. Gerber's promotion of the franchise prototype was perfectly aligned with the second wave of franchise expansion in the United States, which occurred after the FTC created regulations following the meteoric and bumpy launch of the franchise model in the 1960s and 70s.

Gerber's training system is effective, and many companies attribute their success to it, the most famous of which is the 1-800-Got-Junk franchise.

Benefits of Systemization

If you ever plan on franchising your business, or growing it to multiple locations, or just want to make it easier to run, there are a number of benefits to systemizing it. In the next chapter we'll examine a great case study of a friend of mine who was able to remove himself completely from the day-to-day functions of his multi-million dollar business. His workload was reduced to a half day in the office every Monday, freeing him up to spend time with his family and start other profitable businesses.

Here are the immediate benefits I always see when my clients start systemizing the activities in their business.

REDUCE FIRES

Most owners I know are full time firefighters, walking around every day with extinguishers in both hands, putting out fires throughout their business. It's the epitome of being in reactive mode and being busy all day, but not making any progress since you're just fighting to keep the business from burning down.

By documenting processes and training your staff on how to complete them, the *"got a minute?"* meetings stop, and the decision-making anxiety felt by most employees dissipates. Once you document and delegate effectively you might actually experience some anxiety when you don't have staff coming at you 24/7. The feeling of being needed is a strong source of significance for many business owners.

IMPROVE QUALITY CONSISTENCY

Starbucks has a four-inch thick training manual for their baristas. This is a $9.20/hour job, and involves as much training as a neurosurgeon in their first year of residency*. The result of this extensive training is that you can walk into any of the thousands of Starbucks around the world and experience the same taste from any drink you order.

Once you establish a baseline quality and then price your products or services on it, maintaining that quality is paramount to sustaining your position in the marketplace. Inconsistency in quality is a major bottleneck to growth, and documentation and training is the best way to fix it.

---

* Not really, but it sounded like a hilarious example when I wrote it.

SPEED ON-BOARDING

Fast growth in most businesses requires the recruitment of talented staff on a regular basis. The first bottleneck is always finding the talent since knowledge workers are in short supply in most industries. The next bottleneck is to get them on-board and up to full production levels as fast as possible. Any delay in this not only costs the company money, but it also increases the chance that the employee will look elsewhere for something more stable and fulfilling.

There's nothing worse for a new employee than being excited to start working for a company, only to be thrown into the fire to figure out their job on the fly. That sense of excitement quickly turns to feeling overwhelmed and anxious.

AID OPTIMIZATION

As you've seen throughout this book, you can't fix what you can't inspect. The first step in assessing anything is to document it. So having your processes documented and referenced regularly is the fastest path to optimizing them. It cuts the research time in half (or more) when you are ready to improve on anything.

Another advantage of having documentation is that when new staff review it, their fresh perspective generates questions that can lead to improvements and optimizations. You'll undoubtedly see areas to improve as you start documenting, too.

INCREASE AUTONOMY

I haven't covered what you truly want out of your business yet, as that's in the next section on Vision. But getting your business systemized gives you more options to accomplish whatever it is you want with it. For most business owners, the ultimate goal is having the business make money when they're out of the office or on vacation as easily as when they're in the office. Systems help you achieve this because your staff are equipped with the information they need to do their job without relying on you as their guide.

I know it may seem like a pipe dream to get your business to this point, but documenting the processes is the first step to making it a reality.

INCREASE COMPANY VALUE

Whether you plan to pass this business on to your kids or employees, or sell it someday, documented systems are a proven way to increase the value of your company. There are numerous organizations focused on increasing the value of your business by simply walking you through the systemization of it, removing you from the day-to-day operations in the process.

It makes perfect sense, too. The last thing a buyer of your business wants is to have to rely on you to transfer all of your knowledge over to them after they buy it. You're too great a risk for them, whether you check out mentally or just die. By removing yourself from the operations and reducing a potential buyer's risk, you will increase the number of buyers who will be happy to pay you more for your business.

System Zealots

For all the benefits of creating systems in your business, there are a number of overblown claims made by some in the systems world. The most pervasive claim is that growth is inevitable in a business that systemizes their operations. This is an appealing argument since documenting processes is a relatively simple activity. Unfortunately, it is a false assumption since the real drivers of all growth in a business are marketing and innovation (per Peter Drucker), both of which require significant trial and error on an continuing basis. I have not found a reliable systems solution that supports the kind of experimentation in marketing and innovation that justifies treating systems as a primary goal.

Certainly, there are businesses that are so wasteful and inefficient that systemization can help optimize what they're doing, allowing them to increase capacity and profits. But that is a gain of efficiency, not sustained growth.

Another argument against systemization as the formula for success is that it doesn't solve the talent vacuum for a knowledge-based businesses. Of course, it works for fast food, chain hotels, residential services, and other simple delivery businesses because the goods or services they deliver require little more talent than following a checklist. When you get into professional services and custom manufacturing, you cannot systemize the brainpower needed to solve complex problems.

What can be systemized in knowledge businesses is the recruiting, training, and ongoing management of top talent, since that's a major competitive advantage when the pool of available applicants is limited and competition is high.

Where To Start

So, where should you start documenting systems within your business? The number of choices can be overwhelming, especially if it has a lot of complexity. As with so much of the advice throughout this book, the first place I recommend digging into is wherever you are spending the most energy, whether physical or emotional. That is usually the place that will benefit the most from improved documentation and delegation. Additionally, cleaning up this sore spot frees up your mental and emotional energy, so you are more effective and fulfilled as you devote your energy to more important matters.

A smart practice is to document and delegate whatever bottleneck you are tackling at any given time. The solution removes the bottleneck, and the improvement is sustained by the documentation.

You can simply follow the path of frustration and firefighting to continue documenting the processes in your business until it is running like a well-oiled machine. I recommend this path if you find the documentation and delegation process tedious, since it keeps your energy output as efficient as possible.

If you find that one of your staff loves to document processes and has the time and energy to do so then I suggest moving through this order of priority.

CLOSING

As we covered in Chapter 6 on Closing, there is always room for improvement in the process of converting prospects to paid clients. Documenting the steps in that process will allow you to see the clear improvements you can make, while setting standards for your sales team to follow. You don't need to do a complete bottleneck breakthrough cycle to fully optimize it, as even the smallest of improvements will make a significant impact.

FULFILLMENT

If you have a complex deliverable, you should document the kickoff process since that's the key to smooth delivery. "Garbage in, garbage out" is the mantra to remember when you need the motivation to document the kickoff process, because every improvement here results in ten times fewer mistakes and change orders later.

This is a major bottleneck for many mature firms that experience spikes of growth, and/or new project management staff that don't have the expertise the company normally relies on for this stage. Documenting and training at this stage is critical for supporting any type of scale.

ACCOUNTS RECEIVABLE

Since cash flow is the lifeblood of every business, collecting payment from clients in a timely fashion is vital. When accounts receivable surpasses an average of 45 days, whoever is in charge of collecting it typically just needs some additional support to collect it more assertively.

Documenting the process will show you where you can make simple adjustments to improve the results and shorten the days outstanding for A/R.

Just because your industry may have a standard term for payments doesn't mean you have to follow it. If most companies in your space allow for sixty-day payment terms, setting yours at thirty days probably won't be met with much resistance, and it will give you twice the cash flow advantage over competitors. This advantage allows you to better handle any market setbacks since you have more cash on hand to ride them out. It also allows you to experiment more aggressively in your marketing expense because your cash cushion is larger.

ON-BOARDING

If you want to experience any amount of revenue growth, you will have to consistently hire new staff to increase capacity. Developing and documenting your on-boarding and training process is the only way to prevent recruiting from consuming too much energy. Zappos[*] is a great company to model your business after, as they not only hire a huge number of customer service staff, but they also train them expertly and filter out the ones who aren't fully committed to their culture and vision.

Their on-boarding is a major factor that led to Amazon purchasing Zappos for $847 million just ten years after they were founded.

REPORTING

One of the most tedious parts of running a company is figuring out what reports to review on a regular basis, and how to generate them without taking hours and hours of time. The list of options is long and varied, so the core reports that everyone should be reviewing include the following:

#1 - INCOME STATEMENT (OR PROFIT & LOSS STATEMENT)

This shows how much money you made and how much you spent in a given time. I always recommend doing it on a cash basis, as opposed to an accrual basis, since cash is what you live on.

---

[*] Their HR practices are so effective that they now train other companies how to do it. See more here: *bbg.li/zappos*

Accrual basis is what CPAs and the IRS look at for your taxes, but it doesn't matter for the day-to-day business.

I recommend reviewing this every month, comparing it to the same month from the previous year, as well as the previous three months. A Year-to-Date summary with a comparison to the prior year Year-to-Date summary is also useful on this report to show the overall trend.

#2 - MARKETING

A number of data points in your marketing and sales efforts can take up pages and pages of reporting. I suggest finding one or two key metrics that drive everything.

For most businesses, this is **Number of Leads**, and **Cost Per Lead**.

Instead of trying to attribute the specific cost per lead from every lead source (a great ideal to strive for, but overwhelming to start with), I simply calculate it as:

TOTAL MARKETING EXPENSE / TOTAL NUMBER OF LEADS CAPTURED = COST PER LEAD

Don't worry about amortizing the investment this month in a trade show booth that will be used in six months, since that will be factored in over the long term. Just go through your marketing expenses for the month and total it up. You'll start seeing patterns over time that you can optimize from.

If you don't generate many leads, then use a different metric. This could be **Number of Proposals** and **Contracts Won**, like the civil engineering firm I referenced earlier did.

ACTION STEPS

You should be fully convinced by now that documenting your processes and creating systems around the key activities in your business is required for sustained growth. In the next chapter I will walk you through the step-by-step process to write the steps out and how to turn it all into useful operations manuals for your staff.

Before you read ahead, write out the key parts of your business to build the documentation around.

1. How do you generate leads? Having a consistent process for this goes a long way to driving new revenue.
2. How are prospects engaged and converted? Does everyone on your team follow the same proven approach?
3. Once a prospect is ready to become a client, how do you get paid and get them started?
4. What do you do to deliver great results for each client?
5. How often do you hire new staff? Have you held off replacing bad staff because it would be too much effort to recruit and train their replacement?
6. How do you handle paying bills, collecting on invoices, and reviewing the reconciliation of it all?

Now let's get to implementing all of this in the next chapter.

CHAPTER 11

Delegate, Document & Automate

"DELEGATION REQUIRES THE WILLING-
NESS TO PAY FOR SHORT-TERM FAILURES IN
ORDER TO GAIN LONG-TERM COMPETENCY."

— *Dave Ramsey*

If you're like most business owners, you suffer at times from *Commonsense-itis*. It's a sneaky disease that labels so much of what you know and believe as common sense, expecting everyone you interact with to make the same decisions you would in any situation. The higher your intelligence, the higher the odds you are afflicted with it.

One particular client (whom I'll keep anonymous to avoid incrimination) was extremely bright but he had the worst case of *Commonsense-itis* I've ever witnessed. He projected it onto his personal assistant the most, since he interacted with her more than anyone else in his company of approximately 45 employees.

This condition always results in significant frustration for the infected person, because their common sense decisions are rarely matched by those around them.

My client was frequently losing his cool with his assistant, especially over minor items, such as when she asked whether he wanted store credit or to have the balance of a returned product put back on his credit card. As you can imagine, his short fuse for having to provide extra guidance on such commonsense options made his assistant anxious and full of self-doubt about whether her decisions were the right ones. It also made her fearful about asking for his input and setting off another outburst.

The result was that he went through three assistants in as many months at the beginning of my work with him. I didn't have the experience to offer a solution at the time, so I just watched from the sideline, and I heard plenty of his grief from him over the headache of dealing with "flaky" assistants.

He finally lucked out and landed an assistant who was extremely overqualified for the position. She was a bored, stay-at-home mom whose husband made plenty of money, so she was just looking for a challenge to tackle. Even though she was incredibly bright and could pre-empt many of the client's needs, she still needed guidance from time to time, which triggered his *Commonsense-itis* outbursts. Because she was self-assured and didn't need the job, she laughed off his irrational fits, which she found very entertaining. She and I had some laughs over them, and the few I remember still make me chuckle.

Needless to say, the client was quite fortunate to have found her, otherwise the turnover would have continued forever. I encourage you get to the root of your *Commonsense-itis* instead of relying upon luck to provide someone willing to endure your abuse. Your staff will become much happier and more productive because of it.

The root cause of *Commonsense-itis* is the assumption that your judgment is the default used by everyone else. Since you built your business from scratch, you know every miniscule detail about it, just like you do about your kids or pets. But just as they don't know every nuance or trait of your kids, your employees will never show up fully equipped to do everything you expect them to do in their hired role.

The guaranteed instant cure of *Commonsense-itis* is to adopt the *"eight year old"* management perspective I shared with you in Chapter 7. By viewing everyone in your company as an eight-year-old, you'll stop assuming that they know everything you know. They're a relatively blank canvas, in need of direction and encouragement to learn what you know so they can deliver like you expect.

This sets the foundation to systemize your business by first learning how to delegate effectively.

Delegate

The creed of those afflicted with *Commonsense-itis* is, *"It takes more effort to tell someone else how to do this, so I'll just do it myself!"*

This creates a self-fulfilling prophecy and self-inflicted prison in one quick step. Obviously, this is not something you want to perpetuate as you grow your business and have more autonomy to invest your time in whatever fulfills you.

To eliminate this self-limiting belief (we'll tackle more of these later in Chapter 14), we need to replace this belief with something more useful and supportive.

I like shifting the statement to something along the lines of, *"How easily can I give this to someone who would love doing it, and do a great job at it?"* *

It's a simple question, but I'm sure you see the difference between the problem and solution statements. The first kills hope and inspiration, piling on frustration and obligation, while the second creates excitement, multiplying hope and inspiration making the problem that much easier to solve.

The belief that delegating a task to someone else takes more effort than it's worth grows out of frustration from poor results caused by bad delegation in the past.

In the case of my client, he would email tasks to his assistants with very little detail or guidance about how to handle variables that might arise. In the case of the product return, he couldn't predict the proffered option of store credit or having the balance refunded to his credit card, but it would have taken him mere seconds to establish a preference for getting the balance refunded as the default rule once his assistant asked for guidance.

That one step of adding a sentence or two stating how to handle similar situations in the future eliminates having to deal with it again. Like compound interest, the return on additional clarity when giving directions adds up significantly over time, saving massive amounts of effort when delegating.

Delegate Effectively

Here are the guidelines I recommend using as you start building your delegation skills.

---

* As much as you can't believe anyone would enjoy doing this crap, they actually exist and are eager to help if you'll just ask.

OVER-DEFINE

Until you are completely in-sync with whomever you delegate to and are consistently getting great results, I always recommend specificity. You'll feel like you are insulting the intelligence of the staffer at first. But as with a pendulum that is out of balance, you're simply adjusting it so it swings back to a healthy clarity.

I always add this disclaimer when starting with a new staff member:

> *"Forgive me if this includes some obvious stuff. I just don't want to leave you hanging, uncertain of what to do, and have you end up waiting on me for more guidance. Don't worry about asking questions, as it's possible I've still left out something critical."*

DEADLINE

Giving a deadline for the task helps prioritize it in relation to the other tasks they already have to complete. If you're like me, you're not always sure how long something might take. Again, I include disclaimers here to help get the two of you on the same page.

> *"I need this by Friday at 3 p.m., but if that's completely unreasonable, just let me know what you think is reasonable. If you have other priorities that might conflict with this, let me know and I'll help you reorder them."*

SCOPE

So many employees have no idea what a particular task is worth to the company. Pair that with Parkinson's Law, which says that *"Work expands to fill the time available for its completion,"* and you can end up with staff spending insane amounts of time on the most trivial tasks.

I've had staff take hours and hours for something that I had done previously in under thirty minutes. I was dumbfounded at the wasted time, but came to realize it was entirely my fault because I didn't give them any boundaries.

Here's what I include now with every task:

> *"I think this should only take one hour, so if you're not making progress with it after thirty minutes, check in with me to see what might need to be adjusted. If I'm way off on my estimate, just let me know, and we can agree how much extra time is needed."*

AUTHORITY

As I discussed in Chapter 7, having responsibility for an outcome, but no authority to do what's needed to ensure it happens is a form of torture for anyone in that position. So I try to grant authority as needed during my delegation of a task.

Zappos is famous for giving their customer service staff the authority to keep customers happy. The stories about it are fantastic, and Zappos turns their customers into raving fans in the process.

I suggest extending authority in stages so the employee doesn't end up hanging themselves with too much of it too soon.

With these guidelines in mind, here is a sample task I recently assigned to a new project manager that delivered a great result:

> *"Hi Jessica,*
> *Included below are the transcripts for the testimonial booklet. We're visualizing a 5.5" x 8.5" book with a color cover*

and B&W interior that we can get printed at Createspace as needed. Please double check their printing options for this format. I imagine it will be 50–70 pages in length, so please organize each testimonial as its own chapter.

Here's the specificity, with the print source so she can get the print specs as well as figure out what their limitations are.

Please get the first transcript edited, and then have the first chapter designed and sent over as a proof so we can get it dialed in as a template for the rest to follow.

More specificity, demonstrating how I expect it to be project managed to reduce as much waste as possible.

Let me know if you can't get it to me by Monday, as our target print date is [14 days from now] and I figure there will be a few rounds of edits to finalize it. None of this is in stone, so just let me know if it's unreasonable or not and we can adjust.

Clear deadline, broken up into simple stages.

Also, the budget for this is $850, so please let me know if you need any help breaking this down between the editor, designer, and your time. And let me know if you have a hard time getting the tasks to fit the budget since we can likely simplify the design if needed.

Scope and authority to get it done.

Thanks,
—Josh"

Document

Now we've reached the systemization stage. The sales pitch for it in the previous chapter was pretty compelling. Re-read it if you need a refresher. Without documentation, delegation becomes a hamster wheel of repeating the same stuff manually every time you bring on a new team member.

I don't know about you, but I get bored with repeating myself. And it is such a waste of time.

The first objective is actually not what to write down, but rather where to store it so it doesn't end up lost or out of sight and out of mind. There's nothing more infuriating than taking the time to document your processes and train your staff on them, only to forget where the documentation is and then have to do it all over again.

As much as I'm a fan of technology, I've found that an old school three-ring binder that every employee keeps at their desk is the single most effective documentation library available. It starts out meager, with very little in it, but over time it grows to become the operation manual for their job.

Obviously, a file server, like Google Drive, is a great place to save the digital versions of each process outline/checklist, but relying on it as the only reference tends to be forgotten on a day-to-day basis.

The added benefit of a physical binder for the documentation library is that it makes it easy to add notes and review with the employee whenever they can't fully execute with it. Once a document is created, I always point the employee back to it when they come to me for guidance on the related task. I also tell them to come back with their binder if they are still stuck so we can figure out what needs to be added to it to keep it useful for them.

This keeps the documentation alive and relevant at all times, increasing the frequency with which the documentation is used and reducing the frequency with which I am used for such guidance.

Documentation Template

This may seem overly simplistic, but it has helped every client I've worked with to kickstart their documentation. I find that too many managers overthink the format and become paralyzed trying to perfect it right from the start.

The benefits of using this template are many. It will reduce the frequency that key steps in any process are skipped, like when to call clients with unpaid invoices. It also allows your staff to show where they might be confused trying to follow the steps, even with something you assume they've been doing correct for years. Onboarding new staff is much faster when documentation exists that they can reference after they are trained on a process. Finally, documentation increases the value of your company when you go to sell it. Buyers will always pay more for a well documented company.

Get a copy of this template in the resources section at *bbg. li/documentation.*

Once you have a process well documented and can rely on the documentation to produce a consistent result, then you might want to look at streamlining it with automation. Be sure to not skip the step of providing consistent results from your documentation since automating a flawed process is a surefire way to create chaos.

Automation

This is a very popular topic in many circles right now, from replacing minimum wage jobs as pay is hiked by regulators, to using marketing automation now that software and web technology has advanced so much. The reality is that automation can be a fantastic tool for your business, but it has a very clear point of diminishing returns in most cases that needs to be identified before pursuing it on a grand scale.

Just as testing in small, trackable steps is prudent (as explained in Chapter 3), I recommend doing the same thing when setting up automation.

Since you have the process outlined from above, you can start breaking it down into segments that might be automated. You might find that automation within a process isn't always feasible, but the transition from one process to another could benefit from automation to prevent tasks from falling through the cracks.

Here's a great example that illustrates this.

CLIENT ON-BOARDING

You've just secured a verbal agreement from a new client that took a few months to close. Now you need to complete a coordinated series of tasks in order to land them and get their order fulfilled.

You follow the steps outlined in your contract creation process, generating the contract with the agreed-upon terms. You send it via email for signature in HelloSign (*bbg.li/hellosign*), a secure, digital signature application. Within HelloSign, you have reminders set to go out daily to you and the client until they sign the contract. This is your first step of automation in this process so you don't have to manually send out the reminders, or even remember to do them. Plus, you don't have to deal with multiple versions of partially signed contracts since HelloSign organizes it all into one file.

Once the contract is signed, you need to send the invoice as well as an intro email to your client manager who will interact with the client during their fulfillment. Upon signature, HelloSign triggers a notification through a connector app named Zapier (it uses APIs to connect different software, *bbg.li/zapier*), which creates a task in your project management software for your bookkeeper (or sends an email as the task). It also creates a task for the client manager to send the welcome email.

This very simple automation example removes hours of manual effort by multiple staff and reduces the chance that a critical step will be missed, possibly risking the entire contract. It costs a total of thirty dollars a month (fifteen dollars each for HelloSign and Zapier), and you can add many intermediate triggers to it as you see the need, such as a task to call the client if they haven't signed the contract by the third reminder.

As with any new technology, you should double-check that it's actually delivering as expected a handful of times in the early stages before you trust it fully.

An Actual 4-Hour Work Week

The best example of systemizing a business and delegating it to capable staff that I've ever seen was in a grocery distribution business owned by my friend Dale Rainey. Dale got his start in the grocery world early on, as his dad owned a discount grocery store in a small mountain town in California. Given the small community, this private store was the go-to market in the area.

While studying architecture in college, Dale started research-ing the buying side of the grocery business and found a whole world of opportunity. Most smart people with entrepreneurial traits find ways to improve a system. To them it's like an easter egg hunt, with treasures hidden all over the place.

Since groceries are a perishable commodity (except for Twinkies, of course), there is constant activity behind the scenes to keep food moving and avoid spoilage. The store that Dale's dad owned was privately held, so he wasn't bound by the buying agreements of a larger chain, the way Vons/Safeway might be. This gave Dale free rein to research any number of opportunities to improve their buying process.

As he was digging into this world, he stumbled across the segment known as dry goods, which includes items like boxes of cereal, bags of beans, canned food, etc. What was unique about this segment was that it lasted much longer than other goods, especially compared to fruits and vegetables. It also had fewer distributors because it could be shipped farther across the U.S., meaning there were greater opportunities to discover, with fewer players involved. Finally, he found that the large chain grocers had strict requirements that resulted in their rejection of a lot of inventory, such as items nearing the expiration date or when there was damage to part of a pallet of goods.

Dale tried out some of this rejected inventory from the larger chains and found that not only was it perfectly good food, but also, and more importantly, the customers of his dad's store had no objection to it either. He ended up finding more and more of this inventory, far exceeding what they could move through their mountain store. So he reached out to some of the other private grocers in the area and was pleasantly surprised at their eagerness to buy it from him.

As you can imagine, this grew into a distribution business on its own and ended up creating a very nice cash flow business for Dale in the process.

Once he negotiated the contracts with the distributors, the rest of the business was entirely focused on receiving and moving the goods to the local grocers he serviced. The logistics of food distribution from multiple sources to many retail stores was complex. Thankfully he had a process expert "in-house" as his wife was successfully running her retail furnishings store that he could model after. They were both even more motivated to systemize his distribution business when their first child came along.

While out jetskiing one afternoon, Dale shared his best delegation hack with me that has yet to be topped. He told me that whenever he would go on vacation, whatever was on his desk to resolve when he got back would be documented and delegated so he wouldn't be the bottleneck for it in the future. After doing this repeatedly, he had a business that could run almost completely without him.

> Whenever he would go on vacation, whatever was on his desk to resolve when he got back would be documented and delegated so he wouldn't be the bottleneck for it in the future.

He would come into the office every Monday for a half day just to review reports, connect with staff, and keep his finger on the pulse of the company.

In the end, Dale simply delegated tasks and had the systems documented for his staff. Also, little to no automation was needed, since his staff could manage the processes efficiently. So don't think you need a ton of automation to systemize your business and have it run flawlessly without you in the middle of it all.

ACTION STEPS

Getting the first system documentation completed is often the hardest step for most of my clients. Here's how to get an easy win and build momentum from there:

1. Download the documentation template at *bbg.li/ documentation.*

2. Ask your employees to see if someone is interested in documenting the systems in the company. You'll be surprised how many might love doing it.

3. Pick a part of your business that you both agree will be easy to document to get a quick win. If you want to get some real gains, pick an area of the business where you've been irritated by inconsistency and document it.*

4. Once the process is documented, give it to another employee and see if they can complete the tasks following only the instructions provided. Add more detail as necessary.

5. Rinse and repeat for the critical functions in your business that you noted at the end of Chapter 10.

---

* This is the beginning of the *Frustration Fix Framework* coming in Chapter 13.

6. Create binders for each employee and put the processes they are responsible for inside for easy reference.

After documenting many of the processes, brainstorm answers to the following questions with your team to keep getting more efficiency out of them:

1. What tasks and responsibilities can be delegated to lower level employees or outsourced completely?
2. What tasks can be automated? Reduce manual re-entry and eliminate delays waiting on someone that can be handled by a software trigger.

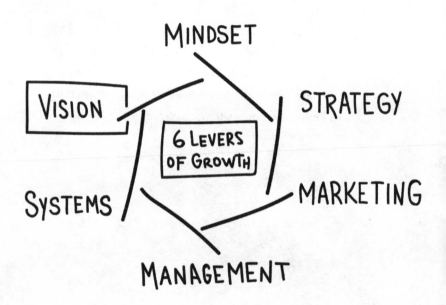

Vision

> "IF YOU ARE WORKING ON SOMETHING
> EXCITING THAT YOU REALLY CARE ABOUT,
> YOU DON'T HAVE TO BE PUSHED. THE VISION
> PULLS YOU."
>
> — *Steve Jobs*

Before you dive in to create your Bottleneck Breakthrough Plan in Chapter 13, I recommend spending some time refreshing your ultimate goal for your business.

There are any number of reasons why you became an entrepreneur and took on the Herculean effort of creating a successful business. Your purpose and vision was a powerful source of energy to drive you then.

If you have lost that vision or purpose, or find yourself buried by the mountain of demands and can't see an end in sight, then you likely need a new vision to pull you forward like a magnet. You might also find yourself in a situation you never expected, with less than ideal options to choose from as you think about what you really want now.

Regardless of what has happened up to this point, going through the next chapter to do some Zero-Based Thinking (from Chapter 3) about what you really want out of your business is in order. Then use that updated vision to dive into Chapter 13 and create your Bottleneck Breakthrough Plan with even more energy and intention than you started this book with.

CHAPTER 12

What's The Goal?

"CAT: WHERE ARE YOU GOING?
ALICE: WHICH WAY SHOULD I GO?
CAT: THAT DEPENDS ON WHERE YOU ARE GOING.
ALICE: I DON'T KNOW.
CAT: THEN IT DOESN'T MATTER WHICH WAY
YOU GO."

— *Lewis Carroll, Alice in Wonderland*

In 1972, at the age of 50, my grandfather Larry and two of his teaching buddies, Art and Hal, started an educational game company. It was more of a hobby than a serious business, as they all loved the creative process and wanted to innovate methods to improve education. They ran the production and fulfillment out of my grandfather's garage as they tested the games in their classrooms and at workshops in the area.

After a couple years of toying around with it, they could see that they had something viable that deserved more attention and effort. They rented a warehouse and office and started selling the games through educational retailers all over the nation.

Since they were all still happily teaching, their primary goal for the company was to provide a secure retirement for themselves, as well as to provide jobs for college students, friends and family members. They also continued to be on the cutting edge of new products for K-12 educators.

Art was the business brain of the team, having a PhD from Stanford. In the early '80s, on the heels of the Employment Retirement Income Security Act (ERISA) that passed in 1974, Art saw an opportunity to develop a retirement plan that could be greater than what they were all expecting from their individual teaching careers.

With these goals, they reached $1.4 million in revenue by 1986 and $3.4 million by 1992. The profits from this revenue provided a solid foundation for Art to manage their retirement plans, growing the investments significantly through the boom during the '90s.

Their stable revenue provided worthwhile jobs for those who maintained it, and their games continued to influence education across the nation. Their goals had been fully achieved.

Then in 1997 my grandfather died of a heart attack. Over the following years, it became apparent that he had been the community builder and peacekeeper in the organization. Add the negative impact on the educational industry of the dot-com bust in 2001, and the effects of decades of nepotism that was never managed properly, and the company's success began to decline.

In 2005 the remaining partners realized that sales weren't bouncing back as well as hoped, so they held a meeting to evaluate their options. During the meeting the founders confirmed that the goals they had set out to accomplish had been met, but keeping the company going would require too much of an overhaul. It was time to move on, so they opted to liquidate the company.

Looking Back

My grandfather's company was a success because it achieved the goals they set for it. Unfortunately, it was only a fraction of what it could have become given the other companies in the education field that had started around the same time and which grew into the tens of millions in revenue.

The educational industry community was tight-knit. Our company was well respected, which opened doors to many conversations that gave us insight into how competitors were unlocking their meteoric growth. Even with this insight, once the company came up against the $3 million plateau, it was intentionally prevented from growing past a certain level.

There are a number of reasons it wasn't allowed to grow, all of which stem from limiting beliefs (again, we'll cover these in the next section). In light of this, the following poem, "My Wage" by Jessie B. Rittenhouse, seems especially relevant when looking at your goals for your company.

> *"I bargained with Life for a penny,*
> *And Life would pay no more,*
> *However, I begged at evening*
> *When I counted my scanty store.*
> *For Life is a just employer,*
> *He gives you what you ask,*

But once you have set the wages,
Why, you must bear the task.
I worked for a menial's hire,
Only to learn, dismayed,
That any wage I had asked of Life,
Life would have willingly paid."

I was too young to be involved in the company when it had the most growth potential since my grandfather died a week after I graduated high school. If we'd had the chance, I know we would have had a blast growing it together.

Before we get to your goals for your company, let's cover some common hang-ups I see business owners get stuck on.

Owning A Job

The vast majority of business owners today simply own a job from which they can never be fired. I first saw this piece of wisdom in Robert Kiyosaki's book *Cashflow Quadrant,* where he shows the difference between being self-employed and being a business owner.

The business owner has a system that works for him to create wealth, while the self-employed person has a never-ending list of tasks they must do to keep revenue coming in. Good thing you have some tools to start building systems from the last section now!

When you look around the business world, you'll recognize that all but a few business owners fall under Kiyosaki's definition of being self-employed. It applies equally to the local retail shop where the owner has to show up to manage it every day, the professional services firm where the owners are the main fulfillment team, and the software company that relies on the owner as the rainmaker to keep bringing in profitable clients.

Michael Gerber set a great goal for business owners in *The E-Myth Revisited*: to move up from being the technicians who fulfill clients, and beyond the managers who support and guide the technicians, to become the entrepreneur that sets the vision and direction of the company. I think that on a day-to-day basis, that's a great goal to shoot for, but there's actually more to owning a business than just figuring out what you want to do each day.

Opportunity Cost

As I mentioned in Chapter 9, every great leader I've ever known or studied chose not to shy away from confrontation. And every wealthy person I've ever known* is very familiar with, and fully aware of, the concept of opportunity cost.

It is defined as *"the loss of potential gain from other alternatives when one alternative is chosen."*

Knowing the "hard cost" of what it takes to run your business is relatively easy. This is the cash that comes out of your pocket every day. This figure also makes it very easy to evaluate and make decisions since you feel the impact of that money coming out of your pocket every time you pay for something, whether it's rent, payroll, insurance, etc.

Every day you are continually choosing actions that prevent

---

* I arbitrarily set the standard of "wealthy" at a net worth of more than $10 million. I find there are plenty of people that inadvertently built up a couple million, and enough "savers" get to $1 million that they don't share the mindset of the truly wealthy.

you from being able to choose another action. This is NOT some-thing to become neurotic about, constantly paralyzed by fear of missing out on something more worthwhile. But it is definitely something to start incorporating into your decision-making process.

The concept of opportunity cost can be more of a challenge to grasp at first, so let's use a common example you might be familiar with.

HIRING

A mountain of data shows that there is a tremendous opportu-nity cost throughout the recruitment and hiring of staff in any business.

You know the hard cost of what you spend on ads on job boards, or using a recruiter who has a clear fee associated with their results. Then you have the salary, benefits, and taxes of the new hire, as well as any equipment or tools you might need to purchase for them. Even with all of those expenses, I guarantee that the opportunity cost of hiring someone is far greater than the hard costs it requires, especially in the areas below.

YOUR TIME

Unless you have an HR department that does all the vetting, hiring, and training of staff, you're involved in the process. Every minute you spend reviewing resumes, doing interviews, and negotiating their earnings package takes time away from other revenue-generating activity.*

---

* You could very well have the long term perspective that recruiting is your way to scaled growth, which is awesome. Just know that you must have sufficient cash flow and profits to commit to this long game.

ON-BOARDING

No new hire hits the ground running from day one. So they need to be trained and supported until they're up to speed and capable of doing their job without constant oversight. This time is very costly because it doesn't generate revenue or keep current operations running while it is being done.

PERFORMANCE

This is where the largest amount of opportunity cost can show up. Let's say the new hire was only a C-level player; they make mistakes frequently, but they try hard, so you have a difficult time challenging them to step up their performance. Their mistakes require a lot of error correction by you or other staff, pulling others away from their own activities. Then one of their mistakes ends up costing you a client, because they simply dropped the ball and the client never got a notification that their order was going to be delayed, leaving them in a bind when they didn't have it for their project.

In sales roles, the opportunity cost of low-performing hires is the difference between hitting or exceeding quotas and always putting up with excuses of underperformance. That could change the trajectory of your growth from achieving 30 to 40 percent each year, down to 5 to 15 percent instead. If this happens in a $10 million company, that's a cost of millions of dollars in lost revenue and potentially tens of millions in lost value when selling the company in the future.

TURNOVER

The worst outcome arises when you keep poor performers on the team as the opportunity cost continues compounding, in comparison to the growth you would realize if you replaced them with a better performer. So, eventually you end up letting them go because you see that it's just not worth the cost of having them around. This restarts the entire hiring cycle and further delays the gains you should have made during the time you employed them.

If you were quick and let them go after only six months, you might have $40,000 in hard costs for their recruitment, salary, and training. The opportunity cost to your company would be in the neighborhood of $400,000. This accrues from continuous underperformance and taking your time (and that of others) away from other revenue-generating activities, as well as the chance of losing clients because the employee let their responsibilities fall through the cracks.

This is based on data that show that the opportunity cost of a bad hire is ten times your hard costs.[*]

Your Goal

You started your business for a very clear reason. Nobody just falls into a profitable business, waking up years later wondering how it happened. The effort and risk involved to get it up and running is too great for anyone to do it without intention.

Whatever your original goal, you are here now, and it's time

---

[*] The solution to all of these hiring related opportunity costs is to develop a robust recruiting system that goes beyond the default job board + resume process. Get help with it at *bbg.li/recruiting*

to revive it to best serve you now.

Let's begin at the end and define an amazing outcome that would leave you awestruck.

Are you like Tim from the first chapter, who sees the best outcome as growing the business so you can sell it as soon as you can walk away with enough money to never have to worry about income again? If so, I've found that number to be a minimum of $5 million today. Anything less, and taxes and inflation can erode it, limiting your lifestyle enough that you'll feel restricted and have to start something else.

Or maybe you love your business like my client Teresa and just want to keep increasing its profits and streamlining the systems so you can take as much time off as you want. Then you can sell it anytime you want as you near the end of your working life.

Whatever the goal, define it now. The more specificity, the better. Put a timeline on it. Play around with different timelines until you find one that makes you feel both excited and at peace. Excitement with anxiety means the timeline isn't quite right for you and will create resistance as you try to achieve it.

Don't focus on minutiae like what you'll do on a daily basis, but rather what you want to accomplish with the business, both financially and charitably, and what level of autonomy or free time you want to get from it.

And don't worry about this goal being set in stone. You can always update it and let it evolve as you continue to evolve as a business owner. As the profit grows, you may find yourself like a friend of mine who limits her income to $300,000 and stashes the rest in various long-term assets.

Or maybe you'll end up with so much time off that you'll start investing the surplus profits in flipping classic Ferraris like another friend of mine.

If you find that you've been so mentally trapped by your business that you can't think of an inspiring goal, you need a recharge. I always suggest taking some time off to fill your emotional tank. For me, it's doing something active with friends, like riding my motorcycle or playing tennis. It might mean sitting on the beach and reading a book for half a day, or renting a hotel room and just getting room service and watching a movie and sleeping in the next day.

Whatever gets you recharged, make space to do it. That's the only way you'll come up with a worthwhile vision for your business that actually inspires and excites you.

Define Reality

Like the Alice in Wonderland quote that opened this chapter, if you don't know where you want to end up, it doesn't really matter which way you go. And without knowing where you are currently, there's no way to know how to get to your destination.

So you need to take some time to define where your business is today before you can make the plan to bring your vision into reality.

1. What's your revenue? If it's fluctuating, just look at the last six months.
2. What about profits? Get the actual dollar amount, as well as the percentage of total revenue.
3. What about your income and net worth? Are they

stagnant or growing?

4. How are your staff performing? All-Stars or Bad News Bears?

5. Do you like your clients? Do you wake up worrying about them or are you excited to work with them?

6. Is your industry growing or taking a beating? Are there clear opportunities you can exploit in the market?

7. How stressed out are you running your business? Be honest. Nobody is judging you.

8. How much time are you spending running it every week?

9. What are you missing out on that you'd rather be doing? Are you deferring life for some reason?

10. How's your marriage? Are you using the business as an excuse to avoid investing in your spouse?

Work Backwards

Now that you have a vision that gets your business to serve you as much as possible, and also have an assessment on your current status, the next step is to fill in the gap. This is best done by working backwards to define rough stages that help close the gap. You're not going to know exactly what to do at each stage, and you will need to adjust as you move forward, so just start sketching out your ideas for each stage. They will get more polished as you continue this process.

You might have to do some research before you fill in the gaps to make sure you know the key factors you need in place to make the goal feasible.

Tim found the larger companies in his industry would pay around six times EBITDA for a company his size. After paying off their equipment debt and splitting it between his two partners, he found that they needed about 30 percent more revenue to hit the magic number. This is a tremendous insight that will help him fill in the gap between where they are and where they want to be.

The beauty is that this entire book is built to help you fill in the gaps at every stage that comes up. We'll get into how to start doing it in the next chapter. Before we do that, here's one more nugget to help you stay on track with your vision and goals.

Seddon Days

In July 2015 I had the privilege of attending a webinar with a guy from the U.K. named Mike Seddon that transformed my life, and that of many others. Mike had just found out that he had only weeks to live, as he had been diagnosed with an inoperable and incurable cancer. A friend suggested doing this webinar since he was very much at peace with his mortality and felt he had some wisdom worth passing on.

Mike put together the webinar in which he covers five key questions he asked himself regularly during days he would take off to reflect on his life. From these questions he found clear actions he needed to take to continually improve his life and step more completely into his most fulfilling purpose.

After the webinar, attendees started taking a day off to reflect and take action, calling them "Seddon Days" in honor of Mike.

Watch the hour-long webinar here: *bbg.li/seddon*

Do it tonight with your spouse. I can't think of anything more significant for you.

Here are the five key questions for future reference as you take your Seddon Days:

1. What is my why?
2. What does success look like?
3. Am I enjoying the journey?
4. Am I hanging out with the right people?
5. What would happen to my loved ones?

ACTION STEPS

Regardless of how clear you are on your ultimate goal for the business, I strongly recommend the following tune-up before you dive in to tackle bottlenecks in the next chapter.

1. Go back a couple pages to answer the questions to define your reality as it is today.
2. Carve out an hour and watch the Seddon Days webinar at *bbg.li/seddon* and answer the five questions above.
3. Devote at least 30 minutes without distraction to sketch out some notes on what an inspiring final goal could be for your business. Don't judge what comes out, just let it flow.
4. Look at where you want the business to go and compare it to the answers in step 1 that define reality today. This gap will help you find and fix your biggest bottlenecks in the next chapter to get to your ultimate goal.

CHAPTER 13

Bottleneck Breakthrough Plan

"THE REACTIONARY OWNER EARNS A SALARY,
WHILE THE PROACTIVE OWNER BUILDS ASSETS."

—Joshua Long

Congratulations! You have invested more effort than many of your peers to get to this point of the book. I hope you found useful insights and strategies throughout that will make you a better business owner and help you unlock new growth by finding and fixing your bottlenecks.

My goal with this chapter is to reward you for the hard work of getting here. Now, we'll build on what you learned in the previous chapters, pulling together all of your notes from the Action Steps so you can develop your Bottleneck Breakthrough Plan to implement immediately.*

Before we dig into how to develop your implementation plan, remember that there's no perfect way to do this. It also means there's no wrong way to go about it either. Imperfect action is always better than perfectly planned inaction.

---

* Want a shortcut? Go to *bbg.li/assessment* and take the Bottleneck Breakthrough Assessment.

So don't worry about getting it "right" or missing something that might be critical down the road. The results will produce compound returns as you continue to execute, regardless of which order you implement them in. Only good things will come from moving forward.

Quick Wins

When I worked for Chet Holmes, the sales and marketing overhaul he prescribed for our clients was a massive undertaking. The strategy was always brilliant, upgrading their messaging and closing process in a big way, but it took forever to implement. Six months was the average timeline, and all but the largest and most committed clients would grow weary.

It was a dilemma, because we knew it would work, but we couldn't give the clients a shot of willpower to keep them fully engaged long enough to let it achieve its full potential.

While at lunch with Jay Abraham during this time, I asked him about this endurance challenge since he had worked closely with Chet for years. Jay gave me an insight that has been the backbone of my consulting ever since, and it's a big reason I was able to develop the *Bottleneck Breakthrough Method* and deliver results so effectively.

Jay told me that as a consultant he learned early on that getting quick wins for clients is the most important goal. Once an owner sees an improvement in any part of their business, their motivation, endurance, and willpower is instantly boosted. This also creates an environment in which the owner can handle the larger changes that will be necessary later.

It is also a win-win situation, since the business owner

gets a rapid return on their investment in the consultant and his plan.

As you develop your plan, my recommendation is to start with something small that will produce a quick win for you. Consider stringing together a few small bottleneck break-throughs to build momentum and confidence in the process before tackling a big bottleneck. As business owners, many of us suffer from wild optimism (which is generally a great trait), but it can lead to disappointment if things don't unfold as expected. That's the last thing I want to happen for you.

FAST START

Here are some quick wins that you can start with.

WEEKLY IMPLEMENTATION MEETINGS

Go back to Chapter 8 and start having weekly meetings one-on-one with each of your direct reports. If you have managers, meet with them, and have them meet with the people who report directly to them.

Every client that has ever done this has raved about all the improvements that come from it. It seems like such a trivial activity, but it makes a huge difference. Re-read Chapter 8 if you need convincing to get started with it.

DOCUMENT

Another simple action that will get you a quick win is to have every employee document one key activity they are responsi-ble for. When you review the checklist they create from it, I guarantee you'll see things that are unnecessary or missing items that they should have been doing all along.

Documenting what is already being done in your business supports your efforts to assess where big bottlenecks might exist later on, too.

DRAW YOUR FUNNEL

This is another step that is foundational for uncovering bottlenecks. Generating leads and closing them is the most important function in your business, so inspecting it always pays off. Go back to Chapter 4 to walk through drawing your funnel if you need help with it.

Frustration Fix Framework

Other than the quick wins suggested above, there are two proven paths to finding and fixing bottlenecks in your business. My favorite place to start is with the *Frustration Fix Framework*. At its core, it trusts that your intuition is accurate in identifying what needs to happen in your business. When bottlenecks are blocking that from happening, the result is frustration. Over time, unresolved frustration turns to apathy, which is a fatal problem if not fixed.

At the surface level, reducing your frustration on a day-to-day basis increases your odds of being happy, pleasant, and fun to work with. It also makes you a better family member once you leave the office.

Below the surface, eliminating your frustration removes the mental block when you're in that state. Your ability to be strategic, to generate innovative solutions, and maintain a clear vision for the future are all improved when you eliminate frustration.

At the deepest level, your attitude acts like a magnet to everything around you. Stay in a frustrated state, and you'll attract more frustration and more people that feed off that frustration. Removing it will gain you peace of mind, and you'll start attracting people that feed off that inner peace. This in turn will produce better outcomes.

The first step to finding bottlenecks from this approach is to simply identify all the places you are frustrated in your business.

Be specific. Don't just say broad generalities like, "We aren't making as much money as we should."

Whatever comes to mind, I recommend going through the *5 Whys?* process that was developed by Toyota Motor Corp. It helps you get to the root cause by asking "Why?" to your initial answers, which leads you down to the bottleneck (root cause) that needs to be fixed.

Here's how that could work with the example above:

WHAT ARE YOU FRUSTRATED ABOUT RIGHT NOW? "We aren't making as much money as we should."

WHY? "We've been getting lousy leads the past six months, and they're not converting."

WHY? "We haven't changed our offer at trade shows after Competitor A came out with their new solution."

WHY? "Stephanie handled that, but decided to take more time off after maternity leave, and we haven't spent any time trying to fill her spot."

WHY? "She is the best marketing director, and my partners and I just don't want to replace her and then not have her come back."

This example took four Whys? to get to the root cause and uncover the bottleneck of finding a new marketing director. The advice I would give this client is that they don't need to hire a full-time employee to fill this role, leaving them with flexibility to respond if/when Stephanie is ready to come back. They could tackle the trade show update themselves, or hire a freelancer, consultant, or agency that can provide strategic direction on how to update their trade show offer.

Spend fifteen minutes right now doing a "brain dump" of all of your frustrations (or sources of apathy). Pick the biggest one and go through the *5 Whys?* process to get to the root cause and uncover the bottleneck you need to fix.

You can revisit this process by asking yourself, "What frustrated me today?" Anything that shows up on the list a few times in a week is a prime target to tackle whenever you're ready for a new bottleneck breakthrough.

Bottleneck Matrix

I have consulted with companies across the spectrum in revenue and business models over the years and have observed patterns in the types of bottlenecks that exist at various revenue plateaus. Clients have found these patterns very useful to see that they are not unique in the challenges they face at each plateau, as well as what they might face as they continue growing.

BOTTLENECK MATRIX

PLATEAU	COMMON BOTTLENECK	SOLUTION
$500K	Idle or Confused Staff/Freelancers	Define Key Responsibilities and Assign Them
$1M	Founder Beyond Capacity To Manage Everything	Develop Operations Manager
$2M	Not Enough Large Prospects and/or Too Many Small Prospects	Expand/Build Traffic Pillars for Larger Prospects
$5M	Quality Control	Comprehensive Project Management
	Founder Holding Back Sales/Marketing	Add Functional Management (Sales/Marketing & Finance)
$10M	Losing Proposals or Missing Opportunities	Develop Niche Specialization Teams
	Sales/Marketing Team Overwhelm	Add Sales/Marketing Support Roles
Any Stage	Flakey Staff	Weekly 1-on-1 Management Meetings
	Sales Consuming Too Much Time	Qualify Better/Sooner
	Lack of Talented Staff	Create Recruiting & Onboarding System

Use the Bottleneck Matrix as a reference[*] any time you want to proactively pursue finding and fixing bottlenecks. You might not believe this right now, but after you go through the *Frustration Fix Framework* enough times, you won't have

---

[*] Solutions to each bottleneck are added in this version to accelerate your efforts to break through them.

many frustrations left to point you toward bottlenecks.

Some bottlenecks appear independent of any revenue, so I've listed those below the matrix to make this a more comprehensive reference guide when you're looking at what to find and fix next.

Want a shortcut? Go to *bbg.li/assessment* and take the Bottleneck Breakthrough Assessment. Your answers will go through the Bottleneck Matrix and generate a report with predicted bottlenecks, as well as recommendations on how to remove them.

It is continually being updated as more businesses get results from using it, so my hope is that it will become a useful tool for you any time you need clarity on what to tackle next to unlock more growth.

Define The Bottleneck

Once you have identified a bottleneck, I recommend adding some detail and context to it as you develop your solution for it. This doesn't have to be a lengthy or formal process since you're not submitting it for a grant approval or the Nobel Prize.

Add whatever level of detail helps you see the significance of it, as well as enough to get your team on board with the need for removing it.

Here are some questions to help you better define it.

1. What is this preventing or limiting? Money, time, sanity, etc.
2. What other benefits would come from improving this? System, financial, intangible, etc.
3. What is this costing us? Both hard- and opportunity cost.
4. Who is this affecting the most? Staff, family, vendors, clients, etc.

5. This is a problem because _____. Fill in the blank and see what comes up to be dealt with.

Identify Breakthroughs

Many bottlenecks can be solved a number of different ways. The most common bottleneck for which there are multiple solutions is lead generation. The sources of qualified leads for many businesses today are seemingly endless, adding complexity to building a Traffic Pillar right from the start.

Don't worry about uncovering the perfect solution to your bottlenecks at this stage. In the next stage, we will prioritize them to show which solution is the best one for your situation.

What does matter right now is to start listing possible solutions, and then defining them in as much detail as possible. I recommend doing this in a brainstorming session with your partners or key staff members. It can also be useful to do this with someone outside your company since they bring a fresh perspective and aren't factoring in emotional or historical challenges that every company has.

Feel free to list as many bottlenecks as you find, since the next stage will help you sort through all of them. You can also keep it simple and start with only one bottleneck to solve for now.

To help bring this to life, I'll walk you through a client example that we will also prioritize below.

When Ben at the Mountain Training School came to me in August 2014, he thought his biggest bottleneck was not having documentation for his staff to follow. His frustration arose from having to tell his staff repeatedly how to complete various tasks, from coordinating course schedules with each student to the logistics of getting all the gear to a course location in Alaska, Patagonia, or Spain.

While documentation seemed like a logical place to start, I still took him through the Bottleneck Breakthrough Assessment to see what else might exist that was more important to tackle.

Since the documentation covered his fulfillment, I asked him to take me through his funnel to see if anything stood out in generating or closing leads. He had built a very successful lead generation campaign in Google AdWords, having been trained by the godfather of Pay Per Click Advertising, Perry Marshall. Plenty of qualified leads were coming in every day, and at a profitable average cost of $29.85. Having helped Keith Krance, the author of *Ultimate Guide to Facebook Advertising*, build some of his Facebook training programs, I wondered if testing Facebook advertising could deliver the same quality at a lower cost per lead.

Going through Ben's closing process, I observed that it was thorough and achieved a profitable close rate. When I inspected the specific steps, I noticed that a lot of one-on-one time was spent answering questions, the majority of which were similar. I asked if he had thought about creating a Frequently Asked Questions video series or webinar that he could give to prospects before they applied to the school, and while it had crossed his mind, he felt it was an overwhelming task.

Another idea I offered to reduce the time spent on interviews was to add a more comprehensive paid application, just like high-quality universities require. This idea seemed less intimidating to Ben, so we put it on the list.

From this session, we had identified two bottlenecks: the lack of documentation and the time spent on prospect calls. We also had a possible bottleneck with a higher than necessary lead cost if Facebook proved to be a worthwhile alternative.

The solutions for each bottleneck were pretty clear, so we progressed to prioritizing them, following the next stage in the process.

Prioritizing

Now that you've identified some bottlenecks, along with possible solutions for them, you should prioritize them and then start with the one that will generate the biggest bang for your buck.

In addition to the "quick wins" wisdom Jay Abraham gave me, he also gifted me what I've coined as the *Profit Priorities Process*, which helps clarify which bottlenecks to pursue first, and which ones to get to later, or not at all.

The *Profit Priorities Process* involves estimating the factors involved in pursuing each bottleneck fix. Adding up the values of each factor gives each bottleneck its own priority score. A higher score means it's a higher priority.

Use these five questions to evaluate each bottleneck solution. I've provided a client example at the end so you can see how it comes together.

1. **Time to implement: "How quickly can we implement this?"** The faster you can get this done, the better, which equals a higher score. A long timeline equals 1, while a short timeline equals 10.

2. **Effort to Implement: "How easy will this be to complete?"** This factor is largely underestimated and often comes with an opportunity cost since you could be completing something else. If there is a high likelihood of you or your staff suffering burnout, then the score would be close to 1.

3. **Cost to Implement: "How low can we start the budget to see if this will work?"** This is an inverted scale, since zero capital would be a high score, while significant capital would be a low score. I always recommend fixing bottlenecks with cash on hand, even when the likelihood of success (factor #5) is high, since adding debt for a failed solution is like rubbing salt in the wound. Your cost scale is going to be completely subjective, based on your cash position, risk tolerance, and current profitability to replenish it if it doesn't pay off.

4. **Profit Potential: "What is the profit upside, based on the hard cost to implement this solution?"** Think of the company-wide effects this solution will have on your revenue and profit over the next year, then compare it to the cost of fixing it.

5. **Likelihood of Success: "What are the odds we will achieve the expected outcome?"** Your track record of successfully implementing new efforts will give you a sober perspective when you apply a value. Until you have that to count on, I suggest cutting your estimate of success in half since we're all too optimistic about new things working out.

PROFIT PRIORITIES

FACTORS	BOTTLENECK SOLUTIONS		
	STREAMLINE CLOSING	REDUCE LEAD COST	CREATE TRAINING MATERIALS
1 TIME TO IMPLEMENT (SLOW=1, FAST=10)	7 (<30 DAYS)	6 (30-45 DAYS)	5 (60 DAYS)
2 EFFORT TO IMPLEMENT (HARD=1, EASY=10)	8	7	4
3 COST TO IMPLEMENT (EXPENSIVE=1, CHEAP=10)	9	7 (TESTING BUDGET)	9
4 PROFIT POTENTIAL (LOW=1, HIGH=10)	8	8	4
5 LIKELIHOOD OF SUCCESS (LOW=1, HIGH=10)	5	5 (MATURE CAMPAIGNS)	10
SCORE	37	33	32

If you end up with a solution that has a very low chance of success, then I suggest figuring out how to break it out into milestones that must show progress before going further. There's nothing worse than spending a ton of time and money on something, only to have it fail.

As you can see, there is a lot of subjectivity to this prioritization process, but that's okay since it's based on your deep understanding of your company, staff, and market. Feel free to massage the values for each question, especially when comparing across multiple opportunities. A variation that might help is to use a negative to positive scale (-5 to 5), which will cause some possible solutions to show a negative score, helping you eliminate them. Or you could set a minimum cumulative threshold value of 20 points before a solution will be considered.

In this example from the Mountain Training School, we took the three possible solutions to the bottlenecks we identified and scored them as best we could. Surprisingly, streamlining the closing process by adding a comprehensive paid application appeared to be the best option to start with. The documentation solution ended up earning the lowest score and had the lowest profit potential, so we left it for later.

As referenced in Chapter 4, streamlining the closing process produced massive returns, both in improving the closing rate of applicants and in reducing the time spent on it. We then tackled the lead cost bottleneck by testing Facebook advertising, and were blown away when we saw leads coming in at around $6.40 each, compared to $29.85 each on AdWords. The quality of the leads ended up being the same as with AdWords, and we were able to get the cost down in the $4.60 range within sixty days of starting, generating roughly 650 percent more leads with the same monthly ad budget.

In the end, Ben was very happy we didn't start with the documentation bottleneck. His management frustration was relieved in the end by freeing up his time from streamlining the closing process. He had the time to properly train his staff on the tasks they were responsible for.

Obviously, it's impossible to accurately predict potential outcomes of every bottleneck solution you analyze, so just use it as a reference tool. Over time, you will see patterns in your assumptions, so this will become more effective as you use it.

I've included a template spreadsheet in the resources section on the website that you can copy to use as your own prioritization tool. I use one for each client and continually add to it so we always have a queue of bottlenecks to tackle or opportunities to pursue. We update their values as the situation evolves to make sure we're working on the biggest levers at all times. Here is a link to access the template: *bbg.li/profit-priorities*.

Planning

Now that you have your most important bottleneck solution defined, the next step is to outline your implementation plan for it. This is fundamental project management, so I always encourage a refresher on this topic, even for the most experienced managers.

Building on what we covered in Chapter 11 on delegation to over-define the task, provide a deadline, spell out the scope, and grant authority, a few other pieces are needed to round out your implementation plan.

GOAL

What is the outcome you want to achieve by breaking through this bottleneck? Add specific metrics, such as "Reduce time to close by 20 percent" or "Improve our win rate by at least 50 percent." I like to include a success scale, since all improvement is good even if you don't hit the initial goal. That might look like, "Anything above 30 percent improvement is a win, and over 50 percent is ideal."

FEEDBACK LOOP

Solving bottlenecks can be like any other new effort, with a high chance of missing the mark completely on your first attempt. Having a review process in place, and knowing that you'll have to adjust as you go to find the perfect solution is important. You should plan to make three attempts at solving the bottleneck before going back to the drawing board. This will provide enough room to get some traction.

A client example started with attempting to build relationships with undergraduate departments at universities across the U.S. in order to generate interest in the client's supplemental study program. We started by sponsoring a department event, which was well received, but was a nightmare of complexity to coordinate, especially if we hoped to do it in any significant volume. We quickly adjusted our approach. Instead, we offered to make a donation to their school if students were interested in the client's mission of equipping future leaders. This generated an even stronger response and was significantly easier to coordinate.

If you are delegating the responsibility of fixing the bottleneck, then add a review of the progress in your weekly meeting with the responsible staffer. If it's a big enough bottleneck, you will probably need to provide guidance more than once a week.

BUDGET

The best investors always set a limit on their losses, which triggers an alert when to sell. It's a great practice to follow as a business owner, because we can get trapped, feeling committed to the effort after investing a significant chunk of change, only to have it drag on forever without any return.

Poker players call this being "pot committed," since they feel they have to keep betting to see how the cards play out after they have put so much into the pot, even though they didn't get the cards they needed to improve their odds.

Define a rough budget and make it contingent on seeing real progress. You can always increase the budget as results come in, but you want to be able to reduce your risk of lost capital if it doesn't work out, for whatever reason.

TASK LIST

Since every bottleneck you fix will require a different set of tasks, you can't make a task list template to follow every time. I'm pretty comfortable with uncertainty and figuring things out on the fly, so I typically jot down the first few tasks that need to be done, and then spell out more as we go.

If you, or the person responsible for handling implementation on this, need more certainty, then you can define as many tasks as you need in order to be comfortable with getting started. Just don't get stuck trying to perfect your planning and paralyze yourself from ever taking action.

ACTION STEPS

This chapter is full of action items, so here is the process I recommend to get maximum results:

1. Start with the *Frustration Fix Framework* and list everything you're frustrated about in the business right now. Use the Bottleneck Matrix on page 209 for possible bottlenecks, too.

2. Use the *5 Whys?* process from page 207 to get to the root cause of each one.

3. Brainstorm possible solutions for each root cause. There may be more than one way to solve it, so include each one you come up with. The next step will help you pick the right one.

4. Take each possible solution through the *Profit Priorities Process*. Download the template spreadsheet at *bbg.li/profit-priorities*.

5. Pick the highest scoring bottleneck solution to start with (or quickest to produce a result), and outline the implementation plan from page 218. Delegate the tasks and monitor results in your weekly review meetings.

6. Rinse and repeat until you are making as much money and taking as much time off as you ever dreamed of!

Then message me at *results@bottleneckbreakthrough.com* to tell me how the *Bottleneck Breakthrough Method* worked for you. It is so fulfilling when someone gets results from this!

Mindset

"Our life is what our thoughts
make it."

— *Marcus Aurelius*

Welcome to the most important lever in the *Bottleneck Break-through Method*. I find the ROI from this lever is easily ten times greater than any of the other levers, and also works to compound the ROI of every other lever you work on after you clear bottlenecks here.

The only reason it isn't the first section of the book is that less than half of the business owners I work with are open to tackling it. Potentially alienating half of the readers of the book right from the start would hurt the impact it could have for so many businesses.

Business owners have a unique mindset, as they are the most risk-tolerant group in society, shedding the perceived security of a paycheck to pursue some problem or passion they feel they can fulfill. The saying that entrepreneurs are willing to work eighty hours a week on their own business to avoid working forty hours a week for someone else demonstrates this well.

In spite of being the mavericks of modern society, being a business owner can be an incredibly lonely journey. You carry the weight of responsibility for everyone's paycheck, along with making sure your clients are thrilled with your solution, not to mention the million other demands on your time and attention every day.

Plus, I find that so much of the drive of business owners originates from a place of inadequacy, a need to prove to the world, and often their fathers, that they are capable and worthy of recognition. This rare combination of bravado, insecurity, and massive responsibility creates a unique recipe to reveal many mindset bottlenecks that are getting in the way of success.

If you take this section seriously and start working through your internal bottlenecks, I guarantee that every part of your life will improve, not just your business. It may seem worse as you stir things up at the start, but in the end you will have more peace, joy, fulfillment, and vibrant relationships in every area of your life. These have been more valuable than anything to me.

CHAPTER 14

Getting Free

"A BUSINESS WILL ONLY GROW TO THE SKILL OR
BELIEF LEVEL OF THE OWNER, WHICHEVER IS
LOWER."

—*Joshua Long*

The start of Bill Gates' success and world-leading fortune is well known. He sold IBM an operating system before he had created it, and then bought DOS from a programmer to fulfill the IBM contract.

What is less well known is that Gates originally recommended that IBM work with a company named Digital Research, Inc. (DRI) since he knew they already had an operating system they could license, Control Program for Microcomputers (CP/M). IBM tried working out a deal with DRI's founder, Gary Kildall, apparently sending three executives to his office in Pacific Grove, California, a couple hours south of their San Jose headquarters.

Kildall blew them off, choosing instead to head out for a recreational flight in his airplane.

Needing an operating system for their new line of micro-computers, IBM turned to Gates, and the rest is indeed history.

Kildall eventually ended up working out a contract with IBM to use his operating system after he saw what Gates had pulled off, but he made another critical error there as well. His contract with IBM was more costly than the deal Gates had worked out, so the IBM microcomputers that came with Kildall's CP/M operating system were more expensive than those with Gates' DOS O/S.

In the end, consumers preferred the DOS-based machines because they were more affordable, and Kildall's opportunity with IBM was over.

On the surface, this looks like merely a missed opportunity or bad decision by Kildall, which Gates took advantage of. Before we get into what was really going on, let's break down the myths and misinformation spread about business success, which obviously includes Gates.

Urban Legends

Countless business books try to deconstruct what led to the runaway success of famous businesses. Whether it's Jim Collins' timeless piece in *Good To Great*, or the many books on Apple, Google, Amazon, and Microsoft, they all try to make their success into a formula that anyone can replicate if they just try hard enough.

These books produce some of the most bizarre responses, from business owners turning into "visionary" assholes in an effort to be like Steve Jobs (we saw that in Chapter 3 with Ron Johnson) or creating open office floor plans to be like

Google. All that mimicry turns the owners into a version of a mockingbird, getting attention through lots of noise, but with no results to show for it.

Really, these are simply urban legends, spreading like wildfire because they are easy to pass along and they appeal to our reptilian brain's cravings for easy results.

After working closely with many successful business owners, and wealthy ones, too (with net worths over $10 million), I see three fundamental factors over and over that allow the *Bottleneck Breakthrough Method* to continue accelerating their success.

Success Fundamentals

The first of the three fundamentals of business success is luck, commonly masquerading as good timing. By getting into a business or market at the right time, the market factors act like a rising tide that lifts all businesses. Gates and Kildall experienced this, but instead of adding to the folklore behind Gates, let's dig into an example from the mortgage industry.

When I started in that industry in 2004, I was fortunate to have two mentors who already had experienced tremendous success. They both entered the industry in the late 1980s, right on the heels of the savings & loan crisis. Prior to this point, savings & loans (similar to credit unions today) were the primary lender for home purchases. But in 1979, when the Federal Reserve doubled the interest rates on funds they loaned to the S&Ls (and all banks), it crippled them.

The result was that the mortgage banking and brokerage industry was created. Both of my mentors entered the market at this point, riding a tidal wave of demand as S&L's continued to disappear. Both grew their brokerages significantly in the '90s, with one converting to a mortgage bank (profitably evolving up the food chain), while the other sold his brokerage for millions.

The next fundamental of business success is leadership, because you can't build a company without others wanting to join and support your vision for it. For most business owners, this shows up as charisma, and both of my mortgage mentors had this in spades. So did Gates and Kildall, and every other business owner that I've worked with who grew their business beyond the $1 million plateau.

Not possessing charisma doesn't doom you to failure in business. I believe it just puts a ceiling on how far you can lead on your own before you need to bring someone else in to lead further. Also, I have seen many charismatic owners fail to fulfill their leadership potential. If you're a reluctant leader who others want to follow, then the next fundamental of success is how you overcome your reluctance.

The final fundamental to business success is mindset, which is based on your beliefs about yourself and the world around you. Of the three factors, this is the only one you can control completely, delivering the highest ROI when you invest in it when compared to the other two success fundamentals.

Going back to my mortgage mentors, there were countless other mortgage brokerages created at the same time they started theirs, but less than 0.1 percent of them ever grew to the level of success that they achieved. They all had the luck factor of good timing on their side, and many of the brokers were charismatic enough to get droves of loan officers and staff to work for them.

From my research, the single factor that created massive

success for my mentors, and prevented their peers from reaching the same level of success, was their mindset. They had different approaches: one had the mindset of a bulldog, with singular focus and determination to get through obstacles, while the other was more of a loving coach, investing in and supporting talented staff to achieve their fullest potential. Both had an army of employees who loved working for them and would follow them to the ends of the earth, so there wasn't one "right" mindset that was required.

Kildall's Bottleneck

Looking back at Gary Kildall's missed opportunity with IBM, a few things jump out at me that explain why he failed to capitalize on what might end up being the greatest business opportunity ever.

First, Kildall was already fairly successful. You don't end up with a private airplane without some level of financial success, especially in the late 1970s. His timing was perfect, placing him front and center in the soon-to-be exploding software and personal computing industry.

As for his initial blowoff of IBM, my guess is that he resented them, viewing Big Blue as the behemoth he was trying to displace with the personal computing software and hardware he invented at DRI. Most likely he wanted to stick it to IBM to prevent them from launching their microcomputers, which blinded him to the opportunity in front of him.

Then, when he did work out a deal with IBM for his CP/M O/S, he priced it much higher than Gates did for DOS. IBM had to have disclosed the license rate Gates agreed to since it would affect their price of the machines with each O/S. Sticking with a higher price highlights that Kildall likely felt disrespected by what Gates licensed the inferior O/S for.

Had he not been filled with resentment and a feeling of being disrespected, Kildall would likely have been able to see the opportunity Gates did, and to leverage it with even more success since CP/M was a better O/S. Instead, the personal computing world had to suffer a decade of crashes and failures by DOS machines that cost businesses untold millions and delayed the acceleration of computing power because of it.

Belief Bottlenecks

If you haven't done some introspection to see how your beliefs and mindset could be holding your business back, there are some effective guidelines you can use to start with.

Have some of your competitors grown well ahead of you, taking some of your staff with them in the process? Whatever your excuse for their growth over yours, the root is inside your head. Don't get cute about differences that you think give them an advantage. Just use it as motivation to figure out what's holding you back.

Another way to tell if your ultimate bottleneck is internal is if you are continuously frustrated by recurring headaches in your business. If you go through the *Frustration Fix Framework* in Chapter 13 and develop the systems to eliminate the bottlenecks, but they keep showing up, then that's a sign that something in your beliefs is causing them to reappear. You might be sabotaging the systems unconsciously, or you may be unable to see that the solution you've created for them is flawed.

The final way you can assess if your beliefs are a bottleneck is if you're unable to break through a revenue plateau (as outlined in Chapter 13) that has been surpassed by others in your industry, or you're unable to get the business to run well without you, if that's your goal.

Yes, each of these guidelines does seem like a catch-all to show that nearly all business owners have mental bottlenecks. They affect everyone, and they are the final bottleneck that stops the growth of nearly every business I've ever worked with or studied.

Beliefs Create Reality

The first step to resolving any bottleneck is knowing how to identify them. Belief-based bottlenecks are some of the hardest to identify on our own, simply because they are so deep in our consciousness. They function like our human operating system, essentially turning us into "moist robots," as Scott Adams, cartoonist and author of *Dilbert*, describes it.

My great friend and mindset coach, Justin Faerman, introduced me to his BETDAR Framework, which is the most reliable tool to identify belief bottlenecks that I've found. It reveals the direct relationship between your beliefs and your reality. In fact, your beliefs *create* your reality. In a predictable sequence of events, your beliefs affect your thought process, which then determines your actions. This relationship shows up as difficulty or effortlessness in your life (and business). The framework shows the interrelationships between your beliefs and your day-to-day emotional state, and the results you experience from them.

BETDAR is the following acronym (with introductory explanations of each piece).

Beliefs: These are the base operating layer of programming in our brain. Beliefs tell us how to interpret the world around us and give our experiences meaning. We get most of these from our parents when we are children, and we add to them throughout our life as significant events and people influence them. They are different for everyone, based on their life experience, and are the foundation for how successful we are in life (and business).

For example, someone who grew up in an upper-middle class family where money came easily and business success was consistent might develop the belief that "Being successful is easy" or "I am always supported."

Alternatively, a child who grew up in a working class family where their parents worked long hours and had periods of difficulty paying the bills would likely develop the belief that "I have to work hard to get by" or "Life is a struggle."

Emotions: As the next step up from the foundation of beliefs, our emotions are directly influenced by them, causing us to feel the meaning we give to experiences. Since we feel emotions so intensely, they prevent us from looking at the beliefs that created them.

Returning to the example beliefs above, if you believe "Being successful is easy," then you will feel more relaxed and at peace, trusting your approach to business. If you believe "Life is a struggle," you will feel anxious, waiting for things to fall apart, and will be stressed from pushing yourself hard to try to avoid failure.

Thoughts: This is the chatter going on in our heads 24/7, and it is the result of our beliefs and emotions reacting to everything around us. This is what Michael Singer refers to as the "crazy roommate" we live with in his spectacular book, *The Untethered Soul*. Thoughts are never questioned, even when they work against us, causing us to make poor, even life-changing, decisions (like Kildall's). Singer's suggestion to simply start by observing our thoughts is a great first step to unraveling the web created by any limiting beliefs.

Decisions: After you process your thoughts about a situation, you come to a decision of some sort. You may be torn about some of the decisions you've made, but for the most part, you accept them as the best option at the time, regardless of how useful or accurate your beliefs and emotions about them are.

Actions: Every action is taken after making a decision to do it. They are the way you turn your beliefs and emotions into your reality. Whatever is down at the foundation is on full display here, reflecting your beliefs every time. Your actions determine the course of your life and the results you experience.

Results: This is where the rubber meets the road. It started with beliefs and emotions, and it ends up with every outcome in your life.* If you are getting everything you want out of your business (and life), then the odds are high that your beliefs and emotions are healthy and serving you. If not, then the best thing to begin working on is updating your beliefs and clearing away any emotions that aren't serving you.

---

* If you are now thinking of all the outcomes in your life that were out of your control, that thought was just triggered by the belief "I don't have control in my life".

The most powerful part about the BETDAR Framework is that you can actually reprogram your beliefs and emotions, upgrading to new ones that serve you better to create positive actions and results.

Before we tackle specific steps to uncover and remove any limiting beliefs and emotions, let's dig into some examples of how limiting beliefs and emotions can show up in business.

Bad Employees

A common trigger of limiting beliefs and fears for many of my clients is their employees.

One memorable example was a client who had a warehouse with staff to ship their products. As often happens with my clients, their order volume continually increased, placing more demand on the warehouse staff to get orders packed and shipped every day.

As we looked at ways to optimize order processing and shipping to better handle the increased volume, we found a number of simple improvements to make. A few of the employees resisted the changes, claiming that they were already at capacity and that the "improvements" wouldn't help. Giving them the benefit of the doubt, we took a look at the workload in a typical day to make sure we weren't missing something. After the review, the owner and I were certain the complaining employees were not working anywhere near their capacity, and in fact were cruising at around 50 percent capacity.

After some coaching from me to get clarity on the issue, the owner confronted the employees. They resisted initially, but finally conceded to the new volume standard we expected of them.

As you might have experienced with your own staff reacting

to changes, in just a matter of days one of the employees started griping again about the workload and became very passive-aggressive. His actions affected other staff, and orders started piling up again, creating a backlog.

The owner confronted him and asked why he was causing such a commotion. He replied that the new expectations were unfair and that he wouldn't meet them. When the owner suggested that his job was on the line if he didn't shape up, he replied with some pretty powerful manipulation.

He was a recovering drug addict, but had been clean for a number of years while working for this company. He threatened that if he lost his job, he'd relapse and likely kill himself.

This was the perfect threat, because the owner was very much the epitome of a loving "momma bear." As direct and capable as she was on a day-to-day basis in the company, she was really a softy on the inside, and she cared for every employee as though they were one of her family.

She felt paralyzed.

While talking with me about the situation, we walked through the *5 Whys?* process to uncover what was really going on below the surface and, we hoped, to find the root belief that was paralyzing her.

Her root belief was that she had to save him because he had nobody else in his life that would.

To remove this belief, we started looking at the opportunity cost this belief was creating.

First, she was subjected to quite a bit of stress by his poor performance. The company wasn't getting orders out on time, and feeling obligated to save this employee was a huge burden.

Her family was also affected by this stress since it weighed on her even away from work, making her less cheerful and present with them.

Second, the other employees in the company didn't like working with this "bad egg" employee. Their job satisfaction was affected, as well as their performance.

Finally, I pointed out the obvious fact that her company wasn't a nonprofit rehab facility and that there were plenty of other places available to this employee if he really wanted help. We discussed that his threat of self-harm was really a psychological attack which leveraged her caring nature, and that he knew where to get help if he needed it since he had gone through rehab before.

This helped her obtain the clarity she needed to confront him again and give him the ultimatum that he needed to either get on board or get out. He saw her resolve in that meeting and agreed to comply instantly.

Unfortunately, his compliance only lasted about three days, and then he was back to his old passive-aggressive ways. She fired him on the spot, and he had quite a tantrum, but she held her ground, knowing all the damage he would inflict across the company if she let him stay.

It was a hard process for her to go through because she really did care about his well-being, but the improvement in the company from firing him was worth the short-term emotional strain. A positive side effect was that other problematic employees shaped up after seeing the owner hold her ground in this process. The new employee in the warehouse has been a major upgrade, more than doubling his predecessor's daily volume.

Bad Clients

An even greater challenge than bad employees can be dealing with bad clients. We have all been in this situation, taking on a contract that helps cash flow at the time, but grows into a thorn in our side because the client is so difficult to work with.

Whether it is a Fortune 500 company that accounts for 10 percent of our revenue and is a big credibility builder in the eyes of prospects, or a needy client who is underfunded but endlessly demands scope-creeping tasks, our beliefs and emotions end up keeping us imprisoned by these clients.

Building on the art of confrontation in Chapter 9 to resolve dysfunctional relationships, let's examine the fears that limiting beliefs create when we think about dealing with bad clients.

As you have no doubt experienced, the threat of losing the cash flow from the client is the driving fear. You are afraid that if you confront the client to try to make the relationship healthier, the client will take their ball and leave. If that happens, then you worry about making payroll and covering the rest of your overhead without having to dig into your own pocket to cover it.

This all-or-nothing scenario you create in your head paralyzes you, keeping you in client hell.

At the core, many owners believe they don't deserve great clients, and that bad clients are a form of penance to balance things out.

Whatever the root cause, the best place to start is to look at the opportunity costs associated with this fear and to get some perspective on all the options you really have.

As I've mentioned before, confronting the dysfunction in

the relationship is unlikely to cause the client to cancel the contract. Unless they're Walmart, you have a lot of leeway on resetting the terms of the agreement to make it less stressful for you and your team.

After removing your all-or-nothing perspective on the relationship, pay attention to the two major opportunity costs associated with keeping bad clients. The first is the stress your employees carry when working with these clients, and the second is the inability to pursue better clients because your capacity is tied up with the bad ones.

Whether you have a high tolerance for stress or not, I guarantee that your employees are carrying a mountain of it related to their work with your bad clients. I have seen it firsthand in companies I have worked with, and it is the greatest source of employee burnout, especially for the best employees. Maintaining relationships with dysfunctional clients increases your risk of losing your best employees, which then increases your risk of losing your best clients, who work with these employees.

When you are stressed out thinking about how to keep bad clients happy, you are not thinking about how to find and land great clients. Plus, you know that your staff is so consumed with the bad client's requests that they can't handle any more work, even if it's with a dream client. So you intentionally avoid adding more clients, causing you to remain stuck and making you even more dependent on the cash flow from the bad clients. Obviously, this creates a vicious, self-perpetuating cycle.

The biggest surprise that comes from confronting bad clients is that they often respect you for pushing back. They are rarely challenged, so they may throw a fit to start, but if you hold your ground and show that you are doing this for the health of your company and to create a sustainable relationship with the client, you will be pleasantly surprised by their response.

If they do end up terminating their work with you, then you are now free to replace them with a better client, and you will no longer be held back by this relationship.

Allowing bad clients and employees to remain dysfunctional is a key factor in bringing my work with clients to an end. Without removing those bottlenecks, the business cannot move any further, and my hands are effectively tied. As you can see, these bottlenecks stem from the owner's beliefs and act as a significant obstacle to growth in any business.

Eliminating Belief Bottlenecks

Now that we have covered the BETDAR Framework, as well as a handful of examples showing how it can play out in your business, it's time to find and remove any belief bottlenecks holding your company back.

You have probably noticed that your brain applies a filter to what it "sees," deleting incoming data that it thinks is irrelevant. Remember the last car you bought, and how many others just like it suddenly showed up on the road? This is what is known as "selective perception." They were always there, but you weren't "seeing" them because your brain filtered them out until you were driving one.

Your brain does the same thing with results in your life that match your beliefs. The brain reduces the amount of data to process, filtering it based on what you believe, thereby perpetuating the beliefs. This is why some people see Donald Trump as the devil in a business suit, while others see him as a messiah. Everyone is filtering the incoming data to confirm their own belief bias.

Since beliefs create our results, the most direct path to find limiting beliefs starts with identifying any result in your life that you are unhappy with. Then use the *5 Whys?* process introduced in the previous chapter to help get to the root belief creating it. Just walk backward from the result, to the action that triggered it, on down to the decision, thoughts, and emotions involved, and you will uncover the belief at the bottom of the pile.*

Once you start digging, you will begin to see how the belief bias is always operating. The first step in breaking that pattern is to look for evidence of the new reality you want. In most cases, this is just looking for the opposite of the belief you already have. This trains your brain to focus on what you want more of, shifting your beliefs to align with it over time.

An example in business is when owners struggle to find and keep effective employees. They believe employees are unreliable, lazy, and stupid, and the performance of their business reflects that. The way to start reprogramming that belief is to look for evidence of employees who have been reliable, hard-working, and smart. The business owner can also read books and listen to podcasts about building great teams, and look for mentors who have built a great company around the talented staff they've recruited.

By looking for evidence that it is indeed possible to find and keep effective employees, the owner opens his or her mind to the belief that they can actually do it. This exercise starts building

---

* This is definitely easier said than done out of the gate. A friend, coach, or counselor is usually very helpful to get you past any blind spots.

new belief structures with an expanded, and more accurate, view of reality. Then, more evidence will come in to support it, which will only strengthen the belief.

A great exercise that goes along with this process is to write down every time new evidence appears to support the new belief that you want. This allows you to intentionally capture the new evidence and to go back and review it, cementing it in your mind. This process has the effect of training you out of the old belief in the process. Your brain will automatically look for evidence of the new, expansive belief that you want.

Advanced Techniques

As science and the personal development world have proven over the decades, a lifetime of study can be done on our mindset. The BETDAR Framework and exercises shared here are an effective foundation for you to start unlocking belief bottlenecks that are holding your company back.

If you find them as powerful as I have and want to keep improving your ability to replace them with positive beliefs, then I highly recommend Justin Faerman's work. His deep knowledge of "hacking" the brain to accelerate results and achieve a state of flow is unmatched.

He has helped me eliminate beliefs, fears, and toxic emotions from my life, some almost instantly, and the results have sustained for more than a year as I write this.

If you want more information on how to dig into the more advanced techniques that have benefitted me, check out Justin's website at *bbg.li/flow.*

Removing bottlenecks based on ineffective beliefs works

together with other bottleneck breakthroughs to create a foundation that supports your highest and best results in business and life. The return is like compound interest, as every limiting belief that is cleared allows you to operate at greater capacity.

ACTION STEPS

Just as you learned from the action steps in Chapter 9 on Confrontation, look for people and situations causing you stress. You most likely have a root belief that is allowing the dysfunction to exist, and once you identify it, you can remove it and solve the issue.

Before you meet with the person to resolve the dysfunction, go through the *5 Whys?* process to uncover what your underlying beliefs or fears are related to the issue. It will lead to a more productive meeting and a more positive result.

Having a friend, coach, or counselor to walk you through this process is very helpful since they can see around your blind spots and ask you questions that will guide you to the deeper issues. You will find your mind racing to come up with excuses to justify any source of stress as normal and reasonable, and a partner can help point these out to keep you from getting sidetracked.

It can be an emotionally taxing process to examine your limiting beliefs, but it is worth all the gold in the world to be free of them.

In the end, you will be in an ideal position, one that very few people have ever been in. You get to create your own reality as a business owner who is fully in charge of your company. The life you create is completely up to you, and the effort you take to remove belief bottlenecks is the most rewarding I have found.

Acknowledgements

If you received any benefit from this book, you can join me in thanking my wife Michelle for pushing me to write it. Without her challenge to "Just get started. You'll figure it out," this book would never have been written. Her support for this project was endless, encouraging me every time I doubted myself. My life is so rich with her in it!

The support I received along the journey of writing my first book is a dream for any author.

Brandon Turner was the "big brother" who showed me all the landmines to avoid after finding them with his first few books.

Zach Obront and Tucker Max at BookInABox.com were both incredibly generous with their advice and guidance on getting the book out of my head and into a coherent manuscript. Tucker also helped me navigate the publishing world with his deep experience. They are total pros, and even though I wrote the manuscript myself, I recommend BookInABox.com to everyone who wants to create a book. If you'd like an introduction, email me at <u>biab@bottleneckbreakthrough.com</u> and I'm happy to connect you.

Mahesh Grossman is a multi-skilled publishing consultant who guided me through the overwhelm I was feeling from all the content I originally planned for the book. He also came up with the brilliant title I would never have uncovered on my own.

Val and Kurt Holmes generously shared their cabin in the woods with me over two weeks that allowed me to be like Hemingway and finally finish the manuscript.

Bill Wolfe at ArgusEditorial.com polished the manuscript brilliantly. He is a joy to work with and is a complete pro.

Shawn Hooghkirk at Graticle.com is a past student of mine at Fresno State who has turned into a great friend. He is also a spectacular designer and website developer whom I use with all my clients. His design of the book cover was perfect, and I can't recommend him highly enough.

I am grateful to the many friends who reviewed the manuscript to point out where it was unclear or could be expanded upon. Sharon Hayes was the first friend to read it through in its entirety and share a glowing review to her network on Facebook. This was the first time I saw it come to life and realized how it could really help business owners.

Benjamin Gorelick and David Horn were the first clients that trusted me enough to let me pursue whatever I wanted in their businesses. My work with them led to the first iteration of the *Bottleneck Breakthrough Method*.

There are a handful of friends that saw my potential long before I ever did, never ceasing to support me along my bumpy journey: Warren Fortier, Matt Nutting, Josh Dehmlow, Imal Wagner, Bob Diel, Jon Cronstedt, Justin Faerman, and Derek Naylor. Without you reflecting back what you saw in me, I never would have gotten here.

Finally, I want to thank my grandfather, Larry Ecklund, for teaching me that the greatest skill in the world is problem solving . . . and for being the best grandfather ever!

Printed in the USA
CPSIA information can be obtained
at www.ICGtesting.com
LVHW091303270923
759483LV00010B/16/J